BATTLE FOR THE MIND

How You Can Think the Thoughts of God

BATTLE FOR THE MIND

How You Can Think the Thoughts of God

Noel Jones

WITH DR. GEORGIANNA A. LAND

DESTINY IMAGE® PUBLISHERS, INC.

P.O. Box 310, Shippensburg, PA 17257-0310

*"Speaking to the Purposes of God for this
Generation and for the Generations to Come."*

This book and all other Destiny Image, Revival Press, Mercy Place,
Fresh Bread, Destiny Image Fiction, and Treasure House books
are available at Christian bookstores and distributors worldwide.

ISBN 10: 0-7684-2374-0
ISBN 13: 978-0-7684-2374-7

For Worldwide Distribution, Printed in the U.S.A.

3 4 5 6 7 8 9 10 11 / 09 08 07

For a U.S. bookstore nearest you, call 1-800-722-6774.

For more information on foreign distributors, call 717-532-3040.

Or reach us on the Internet:

www.destinyimage.com

Dedication

To my son, Noel, and his wife, Dr. Cozzette; my son, Eric, and his wife, Angel; and my daughter, Tifani.

To my precious grandchildren, Lena and Ian.

Also, to my father and mother, Bishop Robert W. and Marjorie N. Jones.

Acknowledgments

Dr. Land and I wish to express heartfelt thanks to Don Milam at Destiny Image Publishers for his encouragement and partnership on this project from the very beginning. Don has given us helpful feedback and suggestions that were critical to bringing this manuscript to publication; and without his kindness, understanding, and patience, it would have been impossible. Thank you, Don.

We also extend our sincere thanks to Rhonda Hamilton for editing the manuscript. Rhonda, you have helped us so much, and we appreciate your constant care and understanding as you have given so much of your time reading and rereading many pages.

Table of Contents

SECTION TWO: ENJOYING FREEDOM IN CHRIST

Preface

I live in Los Angeles, California, but for five years, I worked in Washington, D.C. as host of a nightly television talk show on Black Entertainment Television (BET). During that five-year period, every Monday morning I would catch American Airlines flight #77 to Washington Dulles, arriving just in time for my live show; and most every Friday morning, I would catch American Airlines flight #144 back to Los Angeles.

Countless times during that five-year period, I was asked why I didn't just move to DC, why I returned to Los Angeles every weekend racking up millions of frequent flier miles. My answer was always the same. In a word—well, two actually—*Noel Jones*. Bishop Noel Jones is, in my estimation, without equal on the circuit of today's prophetic witnesses. Then again, I suspect that's exactly what most parishioners think about their pastor. But here's what makes me right—most of the other powerful and prophetic preachers will second my motion. Jones has style and substance. They know it, and many try to emulate it. Following are two funny stories to prove my point.

I heard a preacher in Dallas tell of how he always wanted to work the mic(rophone) like Jones does when he's getting his "hoop" on. He moves the mic back and forth in a quick motion while he leans back and simultaneously puts his hand behind his ear while the organist follows him as he changes key, "hooping" up the scale. And the audience is gone—completely gone. Now that…that's style. Except when this preacher in Dallas tried it, he busted himself in the mouth with the mic, blood gushed everywhere! While Jones was pleading the Blood, the other guy was bleeding the blood! Style.

But what's style without substance? Not much more than sounding brass and tinkling cymbal.

The substance of Jones's messages is already *legendary*—and I don't use that word lightly.

Consider this.

Jones arrived in a city in Texas to preach a three-day revival. The pastor of the local church picked up Jones at the airport, and during the ride to the church casually asked Bishop Jones what he intended to preach that night. Jones told him. The pastor encouraged Jones to preach something else because he had just preached that same subject a few Sundays prior! Jones suggested another sermon. "Nope. Already did that, too," the preacher responded. Turns out that this preacher (like many others) had listened to Jones's tapes, and shall we say, "repurposed" them.

His substance is so substantial, his hermeneutics so tight, his insight so keen, and his observations so interestingly unusual, that young preachers everywhere want to be like him. Down to the suits and matching handkerchiefs. What a compliment. They say that imitation is the greatest form of flattery. But there's only one "First Noel," if you know what I mean. Often imitated, but never duplicated.

Because of his leadership, our church, the City of Refuge, was about to become the City of *Refuse*. That is to say, that unless we built something quick, we were going to continue having to turn folk away. Nowhere to park. Nowhere to sit. Nowhere to stand. And that's no way to treat folk trying to find a little heaven after catching hell all week long.

So Jones says to me, "Ahh, Tavis, we have a problem." I said, "Yes, and it's all your fault." He smiled. But what a great problem to have—being one of the fastest growing churches in America—which leads to my final thought.

At the moment, Jones is still the best-kept secret in the church. But not for long. More books, more television, more exposure. Don't be the last to discover the preacher's preacher—Noel Jones. Hear him, see him, read him, enjoy him, and then pass him on—for the Kingdom.

I feel sorry for folk like that young preacher in Texas who "repurposed" Jones's text. In just a little while, it's going to be hard, really hard, to do that and not get caught.

Keep the faith!

Tavis Smiley
Author and National TV and Radio Commentator
Founder, Tavis Smiley Foundation

SECTION ONE

BECOMING A SPIRITUAL PERSON

Becoming a Spiritual Person

The postmodern world is an eclectic mishmash of varying philosophies and approaches to life. The transition from the modern world to the postmodern world was initiated back in the '60s. While the Cinderella church was sleeping, the world was changing. Truths that were embedded into the fabric of the American culture were under attack. Patriotism, morality, community, theology, and the culture were under attack. The hippie movement was at the forefront of this attack while science joined in the frontal assault. The church did not understand the nature of this change and reacted with judgment and condemnation.

The hippies of the '60s were gradually assimilated back into the culture and moved from protest to sanction. They became corporate America. They drifted from communal living to suburban life. They lost their soul and went back into the box.

In the postmodern world there is no anchor, no foundation. Men and women are looking for reality. Drugs didn't work and neither does the dollar. The world is looking for its soul. In this section, we will explore the internal conflict that comes when a soul is detached from its Maker. He has to get out of the box and find his original self. It is a journey that will take the spiritual traveler to an inward space—the mind. It is in the mind where the journey begins. It is the last frontier, and if we can conquer the mind, we can find our uniqueness and begin to express our original self without the restraint of preconceived opinions and judgments. This is the journey toward true spirituality.

The Street That Leads to Success— Truth From the Book of Romans

In A.D. 386, a 32-year-old North African intellectual, now living in Milan, Italy, was sitting in the garden of one of his friends, over-whelmed with grief and sorrow. This man was one of the great schol-ars of his day, but he was in a battle with his mind seeking the meaning of life as he also struggled with lust and immorality. His mother, Monica, whom he loved deeply, was distressed with the fact that her young son was living with a mistress. Great sorrow had a grip on his heart as he realized that he had no power to break the hold of im-morality on his life.

Sitting there in the garden, his attention was aroused by the voice of a young lad whose words rang in his ears, "Pick up and read! Pick up and read!" At the same time, he noticed next to him a scroll that his friend had been reading. As he picked it up and began to read, it appeared as though the words of the apostle Paul to the Romans (13:13-14) leaped off the page: *"...not in carousing and drunkenness, not in sexual promiscuity and sensuality, not in strife and jealousy. But on the Lord Jesus Christ, and make no provi-sion for the flesh in regard to its lusts"* It was at that moment that a spiritual power descended upon him, and a faith was born within him.

In his autobiography, *Confessions*, he wrote these poignant words to describe what happened that day. "I neither wished nor needed to read further. At once, with the last words of this sentence, it was as if a light of relief from all anxiety flooded into my heart. All the shadows of doubt were dispelled."[1]

The name of this young academic was Aurelius Augustine. Augustine would go on to become the Bishop of Hippo in North Africa, a great pastor, and Christian theologian. His writings would shape the course of Christian theology to this day.

A MONK ENCOUNTERS APOSTLE PAUL

In August 1513, an Augustinian monk who was a Professor of Bible in the University of Wittenberg, Germany, was troubled with his spiritual life. For years he had been trying to find peace with God, yet all his religious efforts could not bring the peace and joy that he was seeking. He had no confidence that God accepted him, no matter how hard he tried to please Him. Troubled by his lack of spiritual clarity, he opened the Book of Romans and was reading chapter 1, verse 17, *"For in it the righteousness of God is revealed from faith to faith; as it is written, "BUT THE RIGHTEOUS man SHALL LIVE BY FAITH"* This young monk could not comprehend what Paul was talking about because his mind had been telling him that God's righteousness judged him, rather than saved him. In an effort to penetrate the meaning of Paul's words, he wrote:

> *I greatly longed to understand Paul's letter to the Romans, and nothing stood in the way but that one expression, "the righteousness of God," because I took it to mean that righteousness whereby God is righteous and acts righteously in punishing the unrighteous.... Night and day I pondered until...I grasped the truth that the righteousness of God is that righteousness whereby, through grace and sheer mercy, he justifies us by faith. Thereupon I felt myself to be reborn and to have gone through open doors into paradise. The whole of Scripture took on a new meaning, and whereas before "the righteousness of God" had filled me with hate, now it became to me inexpressibly sweet in greater love. This message of Paul became to me a gateway into heaven.[2]*

I am quite sure you know this monk. His name is Martin Luther. The discovery that he made that day not only changed his life, but would lead to the greatest reformation in the history of the church. When Martin Luther nailed his 95 theses to the Wittenburg door, he launched revival fires that spread across 16th-century Europe.

AN ANGLICAN'S ENCOUNTER WITH THE BOOK OF ROMANS

In the evening of May 24, 1738, a young Anglican minister ventured out to attend a meeting with some Moravians who were gathering at Barclays Bank on Aldersgate Street in London. This young man had started his religious career with such high expectations. He had graduated from Oxford, where he had been a member of a radical group of Christians called the "Holy Club," a club started by his younger brother. From there he crossed the ocean to work with the Indians in the state of Georgia. He then returned to England in despair and disillusionment because of his lack of spiritual power. As the troubled young man walked into the meeting that night, the most notable event in 18th-century English history was only seconds away. Sitting there in the meeting someone began to read from Luther's Preface to the Book of Romans, where he describes what happens when one opens his heart in simple faith toward the living God.

That young man was John Wesley. In his own style, the young minister wrote these classic words: "I felt my heart strangely warmed. I felt I did trust in Christ, Christ alone for salvation, and an assurance was given me that he had taken away my sins, even mine, and saved me from the law of sin and death."[3] The warmth that was generated in his heart that night was about to set all England ablaze with glorious revival.

At the age of 35, his life was changed, and there would be no going back to the old ways of religion. The direction for his life was now set on a new path—one that would focus on this message of faith in Christ. He would know for the rest of his life that the God who is reflected in the face of Jesus Christ had come down to earth to visit him and had done for Wesley precisely what he could never have done for himself. His earlier zeal for holy living would remain with him, but it would be enhanced with an intense thankfulness for the grace and mercy given to him—a grace and mercy that was not based upon any work that he had ever done, but on Christ's work alone.

THE ALTAR WITHIN YOU

The mind is the seat of all spiritual and carnal conflict. I'm sure that you've noticed by now that the act of becoming a Christian has introduced many internal conflicts into your life. Conversely, one doesn't really come to know God until he or she experiences personal conflict. Somebody might have, mistakenly, assured you that when you come to God, your troubles will be over. Well, somebody was lying. I'm sure you have learned by now, as many people have, that walking with God is not conflict free. Whenever someone responds to the internal motivation of the Word and comes to God, while at the same time ceases to react to the external stimulus of the world, he will encounter resistance and turmoil. In fact, the process of moving from the external (depending on a lot of outside sources) to the internal (depending on God and you) can be chaotic at best. Paul, in the Book of Romans, addresses this conflict as he endeavors to define and clarify the opposing forces that operate to gain influence on our mind. When we come to Romans chapter 7, we find that he laments his own condition:

> "So now, no longer am I the one doing it, but sin which dwells in me. For I know that nothing good dwells in me, that is, in my flesh; for the willing is present in me, but the doing of the good is not. For the good that I want, I do not do, but I practice the very evil that I do not want. But if I am doing the very thing I do not want, I am no longer the one doing it, but sin which dwells in me. I find then the principle that evil is present in me, the one who wants to do good. For I joyfully concur with the law of God in the inner man, but I see a different law in the members of my body, waging war against the law of my mind and making me a prisoner of the law of sin which is in my members. Wretched man that I am! Who will set me free from the body of this death? Thanks be to God through Jesus Christ our Lord! So then, on the one hand I myself with my mind am serving the law of God, but on the other, with my flesh the law of sin" (Romans 7:17-25).

It is in the mind that we wrestle with the spiritual and carnal nature. Because we have the power to choose, we find ourselves engaged in the daily battle of deciding between life and death. *"For the mind set on the flesh is death, but the mind set on the Spirit is life and peace..."* (Rom. 8:6).

Many give their life to Christ believing that all they have to do is attend church on Sunday, turn over all their problems to God, and subsequently, God will keep the conflict and they then get to go home to live free from their problems. Au contraire, it doesn't work like that. We can't just take our sin and our circumstances to the Lord and leave them in some mythical place thinking that this will resolve the conflict. It is natural that when we give our lives to Christ we want to be free of all our issues. We come to Him seeking peace and a refuge from the troubling storms of life that daily permeate our existence. We want to leave them somewhere far, far away. So, we take them to the altar to leave them with God. But, where is the altar if it is not in you?

The only altar on which you can lay your troubles is the altar within you. If God is in you, then He is the one who introduces the conflict in order that when you meet God at that place of surrender (the altar), He can begin to replace those things that have always caused conflict between your carnal or sinful desires and the will of the spirit. It is important to understand that your struggle is not with the devil; it is with God, for God has set you up, through the introduction of conflict into your life, in order to bring you to a place of maturity.

It is God who often initiates conflict in our lives (except for that self-induced conflict that comes from our own immaturity). Since God is in man, when we meet Him at the internal altar, it is in our own minds and in our heart where God begins to replace the sinful desires that are inherent in us. How does He do that? He must replace the old mind with a new mind that will now desire spiritual things. In seeking Christ, one eventually discovers the freedom he has always longed for.

THE WAR WITHIN

It is in the mind where we wrestle with the desires of the flesh that are engaged in serious war against the will of the spirit. When we first come to God, we feel powerful as we open ourselves to Him; and at the same time there is another dark part of us that is infringing on this new source of power. This is when the conflict reaches its peak—the conflict between good and evil, between right and wrong.

Often, God's people find themselves asking, "Why does it seem that this conflict has intensified, rather than diminished, since I met Christ?" You must understand that when Jesus becomes a part of your life, the *Light* that Christ shines on the mind illuminates and accentuates two opposing forces—the mind of the flesh and the mind of the spirit. At this time, your eyes automatically open to seeing the *Light* shining into your soul, and you now see yourself in the *Light* as never before. You begin to see your faults and human frailties juxtaposed between your weak nature and His powerful life that is at work within you.

In order to grasp the extent and energy released in the battle for the mind, we will turn to the Book of Romans 8:1-6 and 12:1-2. But we cannot just step into the middle of His Word to Romans without understanding the context and content of the message of the letter apostle Paul wrote to the Romans. It is critical to note that the apostle Paul was the first systematic theologian. His writing style was sequential and methodical; he developed the problem and then clearly established the solutions. The Book of Romans is the most comprehensive presentation that we have of the redeeming grace of God that has ever been written.

ROMANS—THE FIFTH GOSPEL

The Book of Romans has been described as the greatest exposition of the Christian doctrine of soteriology (salvation) anywhere in Scripture. This Book is regarded in theological circles of discussion as Paul's treatise of the Gospel. Many theological scholars refer to the Book of Romans as the Fifth Gospel. In Martin Luther's Preface to the Epistle to the Romans, he writes, "This Epistle is in truth the chief part of the New Testament and the purest Gospel."[4] This Epistle contains an orderly, logical development of profound theological and spiritual truth. It illustrates ever so clearly and masterfully the plan of salvation and the development of the doctrine of righteousness by faith.

The most evident theme in the Book of Romans is the Gospel. Paul supports his credibility to write this Gospel in his opening words to the Romans as he declares that he *"...called as an apostle, set apart for the gospel of God"* (Rom. 1:1). Proceeding from that point, he declares with great confidence his total faith in the Gospel message that has been committed to him. "For I am not ashamed of the gospel, for it is the power of God for salvation to everyone who believes, to the Jew first and also to the Greek" (Rom. 1:16).

Paul goes on to say, with sorrow in his heart, that this same Gospel was not accepted by all Israelites (see Rom. 10:16). At the same time, with joy, he announces that this Gospel graciously (and fortunately) includes the Gentiles (see Rom. 15:16). It is also in the Book of Romans that the righteousness of God is revealed from faith to faith (see Rom. 1:17), imputing through the Word that righteousness is accessed by faith and faith alone. Paul further maintains that the one who is righteous shall live by faith. Paul returns to the theme of faith over and over again. He positions faith in contradistinction to works, making it clear that faith, not human works, is the doorway to right living. Faith releases a heavenly power that enables us to walk right before God and to fulfill our destiny in this world.

Although some of the truths of the Book of Romans are quite profound in the depth of their mystical and spiritual reality making it hard to grasp the expanse of their revelation, Paul presents God's basic plan of redemption in a clear and understandable way. If one opens his or her heart to the Holy Spirit, He will guide them into the truths that Paul lays before them.

In the Preface to the Letter of St. Paul to the Romans, Martin Luther wrote about the Book of Romans, "It would be quite proper for a Christian, not only to know it by heart word for word, but also to study it daily, for it is the soul's daily bread. It can never be read or meditated too much and too well. The more thoroughly it is treated, the more precious it becomes, and the better it tastes."5

Before we move on, I want to compare the Book of Romans to the Four Gospels—Matthew, Mark, Luke, and John. The four Gospels are historical books (describing Christ's unique birth, His unique teaching, and His unique life) with deep spiritual undertones. The Gospels present the man Jesus and the message that He brought from His Father to be relayed to the world. We learn much about God through the way Jesus interacted with the religious world and the way He intermingled with the common man. The four Gospels establish Christianity as more than a religion—more than simply a rule of life. Jesus came to establish a relationship with the human race. It is in the Gospels that we discover the *"theo-anthropicness"* of Christ—His *Deity* and His *humanity*. It is in the Gospels that man meets God, face-to-face. The One who lived in the face of God now comes to exegete (explain) God to man. It is the person of Christ and through His humanity that we are led into a divine experience where we encounter God. And it is in the historical/geographical presentation of Christ by the four Gospel writers that the greatest difference between Christianity and any other religion in the world is established.

As we analyze and contrast the four Gospels to the Book of Romans, we find that the historical and geographical accounts of these Gospels bring us into the person of Jesus Christ by whom we gain our salvation. In the Gospels we meet Jesus. We hear His words and we watch His actions. In the end we see Him dying on a cross and then, with great joy, we read of the resurrection. In the Gospels we see what He did, but it is in the Book of Romans that we come to understand the implications of what He did. In the Book of Romans we ascend the high mountains of spiritual revelation and begin to see the significance of justification, propitiation, reconciliation, redemption, sanctification, and adoption. If we read only the four Gospels, we will never come to understand the spiritual significance of those actions. That is why the Book of Romans is considered to be the Fifth Gospel, for without it, the story of Jesus is simply another story; but with the Book of Romans, the glorious light of Heaven shines into our souls as we are made aware of the heavenly reality of what Christ has done.

What the Epistle of Romans does is give us a theological and philosophical perspective of the Gospel so that believers can come to know

Jesus fully. We enter into all the spiritual realities through our faith, and we are transformed by that faith.

A Trip Down the Romans Road

In Romans chapter 1 Paul begins to build a solid case for the condemnation of all mankind because of man's reprobate behavior. In chapter 2, however, he directs focus toward the Jewish people and says:

"You who boast in the Law, through your breaking the Law, do you dishonor God? For "THE NAME OF GOD IS BLASPHEMED AMONG THE GENTILES BECAUSE OF YOU," just as it is written" (Romans 2:23-24).

In other words, Paul is saying, "Although you have the Mosaic Law, and you had God leading you from Egypt with a pillar of cloud and a pillar of fire, it does not make you better than the Gentiles." In essence, it is like saying to Christians, "You were born in church, but that does not make you any better than others, because you still don't do what God requires of you." The Jews, whom Paul had in mind, considered themselves not only separate from the Gentiles, but also felt they had a pure faith, and that the Gentiles were ignorant in spiritual matters. They knew they had the truth and were proud of it. Paul saw these Jews as dangerously self-confident because they saw themselves as called to be guides of the Gentiles and that God's salvation belonged to the Jews (see John 4:22). Paul's questions were designed to force the listener to realize that many did not understand God's law, had false confidence in it, and could not apply it readily to their daily lives.

Paul urges that these religious Jews, who think they are guides to the blind (Rom. 2:19—*". . . and are confident that you yourself are a guide to the blind, a light to those who are in darkness"*), are actually breaking their own laws and dishonoring God (see Matt. 15:3-9).

Consequently, in Romans chapter 3, Paul declares that all are condemned; and sums it up by saying: *"even the righteousness of God, through faith in Jesus Christ, for all those who believe. For there is no distinction, for all have sinned and fall short of the glory of God"* (Rom. 3:22-23).

In chapters 4, 5, and 6, Paul introduces justification by faith. Paul declares to mankind that you can no more justify yourself than Abraham could have a child at 100 and Sarah at 90. He illustrates the impossibility of justifying oneself using the example of this double impossibility—Abraham fathering a child at 100, impossible; Sarah giving birth to a child at 90, double impossible. So justification then could not be by works. Clearly, justification is by grace, and *grace cannot be minimized or reduced by sin.*

Thus, evil is not contradictory to grace as it is to the law; indeed, man's depravity makes his helpless evil behavior prerequisite for the grace of God. It is his powerlessness to change himself that qualifies him to receive empowering presence that we call grace. It is because of grace that evil can never *outdo* God's goodness. It does not matter how bad or terrible you are, you can't "out evil" God's goodness.

Just as we are getting comfortable with God's grace and goodness, it is in chapter 7 that Paul introduces us to the struggle that all men have endured. With great pain and sorrow, he laments, *"But if I am doing the very thing I do not want, I am no longer the one doing it, but sin which dwells in me. I find then the principle that evil is present in me, the one who wants to do good"* (Rom. 7:20-21). This "now" brings the believer into the awareness of the quandary that whenever we would do good, evil is ever present. Man seems to be locked into an impossible conundrum. There appears to be no key to solving the puzzle of sin. The apostle Paul confirms here that there is always going to be a struggle; even with the matchless grace of God, and with this enormous power working on our behalf, there is a constant battle with sins that have manifested themselves in the behavior of your flesh. Thus, as we battle with the flesh trying to take on the divine nature of God, there is a fight and a struggle to walk in the promises of God.

Paul concludes in chapter 7 with the great question of the ages. *"Wretched man that I am! Who will set me free from the body of this death?"* and then in verse 25 he makes this triumphant declaration, *"Thanks be to God through Jesus Christ our Lord! So then, on the one hand I myself with my mind am serving the law of God, but on the other, with my flesh the law of sin"* In chapter 8 apostle Paul introduces the universal principle of the law of the Spirit of life in Christ Jesus (see Rom. 8:1-2). Paul first declares that the Spirit of Christ assures victory and makes holiness possible through God's plan of redemption. It is in this chapter when we finally reach the summit or higher level of spiritual revelation as we come to understand that God has given His Holy Spirit to us as an enabler, a friend, and a source of power who will walk with us and help us overcome all things.

ENDNOTES

1. Augustine, *Confessions*, (8.29). Cited from Martin Luther's

Works, Weimar edition, Vol. 54, 179ff, by Bruce, 59. http://www.bible.org/page.asp?page_id=2285#P127_9841.

2. Martin Luther, *Works*, Weimar edition, Vol. 54, 179ff, by Bruch, 59. http://www.bible.org/page.asp?page_id=2285#P127_9841

3. Howard Snyder, *The Radical Wesley* (Downers Grove, IL:IVP, 1980), 26

4. Martin Luther, Andrew Thornton, translator, Martin Luther's Preface to the *Epistle to the Romans in Present Truth*, Volume 12, Article 6, Part 2.

5. Ibid

PART ONE

Out of the Box

How much happier you would be, how much more of you there would be, if the hammer of a higher God could smash your small cosmos, scattering the stars like spangles, and leave you in the open, free like other men to look up as well as down! ...As long as you have mystery you have health; when you destroy mystery you create morbidity.[1]

G.K. Chesterton

The first key to becoming a spiritual person is to get out of the box created by the various inputs into your life—religion, negative words spoken into your life, harmful experiences, failure, and your interactions with people—to name a few. Most of us don't even realize that we live within a confined compartment, but we are confronted with it everyday when we are not able to think outside the paradigms that have been formed in our life.

You will understand in this section that connecting to God and tearing down those paradigms is the only way to get out of the box. Allow the hammer of God to crush your little cosmos so that you can see the greater cosmos all around you. Once this happens, you will discover the freedom you always desired.

ENDNOTE

1. G.K. Chesterton, *Orthodoxy*, (Harold Shaw Publishers, Colorado Springs, Colorado, 1994), 24.

CHAPTER ONE

Surviving the Mind Fields

The stage is set throughout the first seven chapters of Romans for the "Therefore" that opens chapter 8. Paul states clearly that walking with God is not conflict free. And it is significant to know that the apostle identifies two opposing forces in us—the force of the flesh, the law of sin and death; and the force of the Spirit, the law of the Spirit of life. These two forces are always in opposition to one another. It is in chapter 7 that we first find Paul sharing his personal feelings—which is, the law cannot save from sin. Paul laments:

> *"but I see a different law in the members of my body, waging war against the law of my mind and making me a prisoner of the law of sin which is in my members. Wretched man that I am! Who will set me free from the body of this death? Thanks be to God through Jesus Christ our Lord!"* (Romans 7:23-25).

INTERNAL CONFLICT: OPPOSING FORCES

It is critical for us to recognize that the flesh and the Spirit are in constant conflict because the mind of sinful flesh sets its desires against the mind of the Spirit. Thus, the mind becomes the battleground of:

- *Grace* against law.
- *God* against satan.
- *Revelation* against situation.
- *Spirit* against flesh.
- *Word* against the world.

When opposing forces battle within the mind, you must understand that whoever or whatever controls your mind controls you. You are essentially mind. Thus, when the Christian believer begins to battle between the desires of the flesh and the will of the Spirit, it must be clear that satanic forces are trying to control your thinking through your flesh, which is connected to your five senses. At the same time, your faith in the Word of God is fighting the sensual perception of your situation. This is the battle that goes on in the mind.

Paul understood the struggle between flesh and Spirit, and in this text the apostle doesn't mince words; he goes straight to the conclusion and opens with "Therefore." *"Therefore there is now no condemnation for those who are in Christ Jesus"* (Rom. 8:1a). The Greek word for "condemnation"—*katakrima*—means to speak against your experiences. Condemnation (katakrima) makes the believer feel negative about self in the midst of what God is doing for him in the struggle. Self-condemnatory thinking actually causes you to aid and abet the negative satanic forces that are working through your sensual perceptions in order to defeat your faith; guilt and faith are opposing forces.

Paul admonishes us to realize that these opposing forces have nothing to do with where you are in Christ. If you are a believer, you are now "in Christ," and the Holy Spirit is guiding you through and out of your conflicts as He gradually releases you from the control of the flesh. He is also reminding us that we are not to despair or become discouraged while the Spirit is fighting to subdue the flesh.

It is important to note, however, that Romans 8:1 is often used to divide the church into two groups—the group that walks according to the flesh, and the group that walks according to the Spirit. This interpretation adds to the conflict of the mind, because it perpetuates negative attitudes in some church-goers toward others when more established church members view other members as carnal, thus increasing the sense of inadequacy and causing a feeling of condemnation even though they are now in Christ.

A careful review of this Scripture, however, reveals that this is not the intent of Romans 8:1. Scriptures disclose that all believers have the promise, that although they still may stumble and fall into sin's power in their flesh, they will experience ultimate victory over sin as they mature in Christ. Maturity is now defined as the continued process of walking according to the Spirit while overcoming the flesh. We must, therefore, understand that a new believer does not come into the house of God and jump from natural to spiritual without experiencing carnal battles with his sin nature. Every believer has to mature, and of course, has to grow in a relationship with God.

So then "do not walk according to the flesh but according to the Spirit" [Gk. peripateo me kata, sarx kata pneuma]" (Rom. 8:4), is an adjectival clause describing *all* who are in Christ Jesus. It must be crystal clear that the battle being fought in the mind has nothing to do with your level of maturity as a Christian believer. You may be a babe in Christ or you may be spiritually mature in Christ, but the key is your *position* in Christ and not your level of maturity. So, everyone in Christ is walking according to the Spirit.

IT'S IN THE MIND

As we seek deeper understanding of the text, it is critical to grasp the concepts in both Hebrew and Greek; because even though Paul wrote in Greek, his thoughts were influenced more in Hebrew. Specifically, God gave us an extensive understanding of two languages and two mind-sets. The Hebrew thought is quite enveloping when it comes to the mind, and when you widen the parameter of this text to include Paul's thoughts in Hebrew, the word that is most used for "mind" is *nephesh,* and it means life; it means person; it means soul; it means creature; it means appetite; and of course, it means mind. Moreover, one writer said, "The Mind is the only part of man (who is made in Yahweh's [God's] Image) or Yahweh Himself where the emotion, the character, the attitude, the spirit, the control, the reasoning, the creativity (by design or a plan), and where the intent of the heart take place. These are all evidences of the condition of the spirit (whether Holy or not) that resides within our mind."[1]

If you accept these concepts, then in your mind is:

- Your life.
- Your soul.
- Your appetite.
- Your person.
- YOU—the total person.

Furthermore, in Hebrew, the etymological root of *nephesh* is "to breathe, or refresh one's self." This is evident in the creation of man because when God made man, He made a panoply (covering) of flesh from the dust of the ground, which was not alive until God blew breath into the man. Thus, the life of the man is housed within that panoply of flesh and what is housed in the panoply of flesh is *nephesh*—the mind. This means that the mind, which is his life, his person, his appetite, and his creature is directly linked to God's breath. It is now God's breath inside this panoply of flesh. In other words, the soul (*nephesh*) of a man is connected to the very breath (*nephesh*) of God; and as soon as you become a living soul, your spirit and mind are connected to God.

Likewise, when the Lord visited Adam in the cool of the day, He didn't visit his physicality, because his physicality was already given to Eve. God came to visit Adam's mind, which is also *nephesh*. He came to deal with what He had breathed (*nephesh*) into the man. Thus, any time the mind (*nephesh*) does not have the shackles of the flesh it reaches for God. The writer says in Psalm 42:1, *"As the deer pants for the water brooks, so my soul pants* [nephesh] *for You, O God."*

Human beings have a natural knowledge of God; and John Calvin said, "There is within the human mind, and indeed by natural instinct, an awareness of divinity.… God himself has planted in all men a certain understanding of his divine majesty. "Not only has God sowed in men's minds that seed of religion, but has revealed himself and daily discloses himself in the whole workmanship of the universe."[2]

Similarly, prescientific Greek theories, which are rooted in theology, concentrate on the relationship between the mind and the soul, the supposed supernatural or divine essence of the human person. For example, Aristotle approached the concept of the soul from an essentially scientific perspective, employing elements of biology and metaphysics that encompassed everything from the concepts of substance, form, and matter, to those of potentiality and actuality.[3] Essentially, while Christians and other religious faith have traditionally deemed the soul to be an immortal entity that lives on after physical death, Aristotle viewed the soul as united with the living body, and therefore unable to exist without a host—the body. He also regarded the soul or mind as the truth of the body.[4] In essence, initially in God's primal creation of man, the body or the panoply of flesh was hosting the mind, but it was not antagonistic to the originally intended relationship of the mind with God. It was sin that contaminated the flesh and made it antagonistic or hostile to the relationship; thus, now the flesh, because of sin, has changed—as Aristotle would say—from being a host to now being a prison warden.

The "mind" is also the term most commonly used to describe the higher functions of the human brain, particularly those which are subjectively conscious, such as personality, thought, reason, memory, intelligence, and emotion. Modern Greek theories see the mind as a phenomenon of psychology, and the term is often used synonymously with consciousness.

The Greek concept of "mind" is from the word *phroneo,* and it means to set one's mind on a thing. The Lord says, *"Set your mind on the things above, not on the things that are on earth"* (Col. 3:2). We must set our minds on things above because the mind is seeking to operate in the realm of its natural environment and not be controlled by the limitations of sinful flesh. Thus, the intent of the Spirit in its war against the flesh is to free your mind from being suffocated by the flesh.

ENDNOTES

1. Dan J. Love, *The Mind of Yahweh, Basic Understanding Series*, 22 July 2003, accessed March 18, 2005; available from http:www.sabbbatarian.com/TableContent/MindodYH WH.html.

2. Michael Czapokay Sudduth, John Calvin, *Calvin and The Natural Knowledge of God*, The Prospects for "Mediate" Natural Theology in John Calvin, Religious Studies, March 1995, accessed 15 June 2005; available from http//www.homestead.com/philofreligion/flies/CalvinP aper.htm.

3. Aristotle, *On The Soul*, cited by Chase B. Wrenn, *Internet Encyclopedia of Philosophy*; accessed 1 February 2005; available from http://www.iep.utm.edu/.

4. Ibid.

CHAPTER TWO

Connecting to God and to the World Around You

The apostle Paul tells us, *"For the mind set on the flesh is death, but the mind set on the Spirit is life and peace, because the mind set on the flesh is hostile toward God; for it does not subject itself to the law of God, for it is not even able to do so"* (Rom. 8:6-7). When satan sends negative thoughts into your mind that make you feel inferior; he also condemns you and gives you guilty feelings of shame, depression, low self-esteem, and unworthiness. Yes, satan wants to gain control of your mind so he can influence your thoughts.

The question now becomes, "Why is the mind the battlefield for conflicts between flesh and Spirit?" God's Word describes two kinds of minds—the carnal (sensual, sinful, worldly, fleshly) and the spiritual (connected to and controlled by the Spirit of Christ). The carnal and sensual are synonymous terms used to keep you away from God; while at the same time, God is trying to control your mind by the Word through His Spirit, which is connected to your spirit by faith in the Word. It is also true that spiritual warfare is waged in the mind because it is the place where thinking, reasoning, understanding, and remembering take place. On the other hand, satan gets to your mind through your senses—that is, through the sensual perceptions of the flesh; and he also uses your senses to deceive and control the mind.

Hence, the carnal mind always listens to the desires of the flesh, while the spiritual mind is concerned about how the human spirit relates to God.

TORMENTING THOUGHTS FROM THE TEMPTER

Descartes (1596-1650), a French philosopher, known as the father of modern philosophy, was convinced that the mind could be deceived. He maintained that demons could cause ideas to appear within his mind such that he was deceived not only about the existence and nature of secondary qualities, such as mathematical abstracts, but even about the existence of things that involved only his senses, such as feeling, touching, seeing, tasting, and smelling. In order to do this, he said, "An evil genius would have to be deceiving him in everything he has ever known."[1]

We need to be aware that the circumstances we experience do not always leave us without vestiges or thoughts to remind us of our past experiences. It must be made clear that satan wants to fix it so that when you go through an adverse situation or circumstance, you pick up a negative idea that attaches itself and becomes embedded in your mind. On a personal level, satan wants control of *your mind* so that when you experience a personal crisis, you also experience depression or low self-esteem. These feelings then become attached, in your mind, to the personal crisis or situation. If you do not rid yourself of the tormenting thoughts of depression or low self-esteem that are now attached to the crisis you are going through in your mind, then when you have another personal crisis or circumstance, you are more likely to pick up additional tormenting thoughts.

For example, you may be experiencing a broken relationship caused by the death of a spouse or loved one, a divorce or other forms of separation causing depression or guilt. Subsequently, you enter into another relationship before you are healed from the depression of the previous relationship. When this happens, you may find yourself picking up tormenting thoughts of worry, anxiety, nervousness, and other mental tormentors in a new relationship while still dealing with the old tormenting thoughts—fear, guilt, and depression—that have been imbedded in your mind from the previous relationship.

When looking at you from the outside, others may not see all the tormenting thoughts that are now attached to you and are imprinted in your mind. We don't always see the feelings of depression, guilt, low self-esteem, or the scars from dishonesty and lack of trust. The problem is that you can look very good on the outside, while at the same time you can be totally weighed down by tormenting thoughts that have been imprinted in your mind.

It is critical for you as a Christian believer to understand that it is in the mind where the imprints of positive and negative experiences are imbedded. And when you don't erase the negative experiences from the mind, it can lead to mental and emotional disorders. Satan realizes that if he can leave an indelible imprint on the mind, he can use your past experiences and mistakes to make you feel guilty in order to cripple your future.

Yes, satan is always trying to leave imprints of negative issues in your mind, and Paul warns us that, *"For what the **Law** could not do, **weak as it was** through the flesh, God did: sending His own Son in the **likeness of sinful flesh** and as an offering for sin, He condemned sin in the flesh"* (Rom. 8:3, emphasis added). God wants you to have a spiritual mind so you can commune with Him. We must, therefore, comprehend that transformation from the flesh, which is the natural man to the spiritual man, takes place in the mind. Consequently, you must win the battle in your mind.

REVELATION FROM THE REDEEMER

In addition to pleasant and unpleasant circumstances leaving imprints on your mind, satan will also insert thoughts of sexual impurity, lust, and mental sexual fantasies in your mind. It is during these times when you might wish that God would just disconnect your flesh. You might even say, "Lord, if this sinful flesh was not here, I wouldn't have these sensual feelings and desires to get into trouble; so I wish You would just shut down the desires of my flesh." But God does not remove or shut down the desires of the flesh, because these are natural, God-given feelings. Instead, He wants us to overcome, to manage, and to maintain control over our sensual feelings and desires. He wants us to learn to control our fleshly and sensual nature and bring it into subjection to the will of God.

Thus, when it seems that God is not helping us through the situation, He is actually sending the Word (*Rhema*) from His Spirit to each believer's spirit. At this point, the Spirit of Christ is seeking to control your mind. In other words, God doesn't always change your situation; He changes your mind. If God would change your situation, while your mind remains unchanged, then you would still be attached to your mind and your mind attached to the situation, even though God has changed the situation. What God wants the believer to know is that if He changes your mind, then *you* can change your situation.

This is now switching the control of the mind from circumstance and sight to Word and Spirit, and therefore brings us face-to-face with the great controversy of dualism and monism. Monism (Gk. *Monos*, "single"), in philosophy, is a doctrine that says ultimate reality is entirely of one substance. On the other hand, dualism is the theological and philosophical concept in which the body and soul are made of two different substances. Descartes posits, "God created two classes of substance that make up the whole of reality: thinking substances (minds) and extended substances (bodies)" and Descartes proves that he himself must have the basic characteristic of thinking, and that this thinking thing (mind) is quite distinct from his body.[2]

Therefore, when you ask, "Why do I have to fight this battle?" The answer becomes clear: When opposing forces battle within the mind, it has to be understood that satanic forces are trying to control your thinking—your mind. In addition, at the same time you are dealing with past situations and fighting battles, God is giving you revelation. Oh yes, God gives you revelation while you are fighting the battle between flesh and Spirit; and you have to look to God for revelation in order to keep your mind from being bound by past experiences and situations. The child of God does not rely on situation; the child of God lives by revelation.

Thus, your understanding of God's position in relationship to your faith is crucial to how you think, because when you are in right relationship with God, your mind feeds on the Word and Spirit of Christ. And when you feed on His Word, God gives you critical revelation on how to change and control your mind. Furthermore, when God wants to renew your vision, He gives you revelation as He communicates to your mind—through faith in the Word. It is essential for you to understand that you are built in the image and likeness of God. God is Spirit and He expresses His thoughts by communicating—His Spirit to your spirit—to your mind through the Word.

CONNECTED TO THE WORLD THROUGH THE SENSES

In reviewing the third chapter of Genesis, we find that God created man in His own image. Yes, we are made in His image; and even though we are made in the image of God, we have certain limitations. We are limited by five senses, and it is through the five senses that we take in all the information that the mind can process. However, it must be crystal clear that our limitations do not hinder God, because our relationship with Him is through faith, not through our senses.

It is also in Genesis chapter 3 where we find that satan targeted the woman's sense of hearing by speaking with her and then focused on her sense of sight. First, the serpent said to the woman, *"You surely will not die* [heard his voice]*"*(Gen. 3:4). Eve listened and heard the voice of the serpent. Next, "when the woman **saw** [looked] that the tree was good for food, and that it was a delight to the **eyes**, and that the tree was desirable to make one wise, she **took [touched]** from its fruit and **ate** [tasted]; and she gave also to her husband with her, and he ate" (Gen. 3:6, emphasis added). To recap the event:

- ◆ Eve heard the voice of the serpent.
- ◆ Eve looked and saw the fruit.
- ◆ Eve touched the fruit.
- ◆ Eve tasted the fruit.
- ◆ Eve smelled the fruit as she was eating it.

CONNECTED TO GOD THROUGH FAITH

It is critical to note that while we are connected to the world through the senses, we do not come to God through our senses. We have never seen or touched God; we have never smelled God—we don't know what cologne God wears; and we have never tasted God. (When the Bible talks about tasting God, it is metaphorical.) Thus, in order to have a relationship with God, we can come to Him only through faith and not through our senses. Why? Because the acceptance of salvation is based on faith in the Word—Jesus is Lord. Moreover, it is important to note that the Scripture also says that Christ is "to be received by faith" (see Col. 2:6-7).

Similarly, David Hume (1711-1776), Scottish historian and philosopher, believed that since we have never observed God directly, we have no experience by which to testify to His existence or nonexistence. Hume boldly claimed that, "Religion is therefore based entirely in faith, not in reason."[3]

Because it is impossible to scientifically prove whether God exists or not, we must make a leap of faith in proclaiming His existence. As we mentioned in Chapter One, Calvin wrote, "There is within the human mind, and indeed by natural instinct, an awareness of divinity."

Paul declares that faith is evoked as a response to the Gospel: *"So faith comes from hearing* [the message], *and hearing by the Word of Christ"* (Rom. 10:17). Accordingly, faith is heard through the Word of Christ; *it was "through the foolishness of the message preached to save those who believe"* (I Cor. 1:21). In essence, it is the hearing that produces faith, and the faith, which saves is a faith which unites the believer to the Spirit of God. One writer maintained, "Paul evidently looked to the proclamation of the 'word of the Lord,' the message about Christ, the Gospel, as being able in itself and by itself to evoke faith. Thus, the Gospel was by the power of God (itself a Divine Force) unto salvation."[4] Faith then becomes the avenue by which we connect with God. It is also written, *"For by grace you have been saved through faith"* (Eph. 2:8). And since we are connected to the Spirit of God, we can depend upon God's Word to penetrate through horrific circumstances, bad situations, and failures of the past that are imbedded in our minds.

ENDNOTES

I. René Descartes, *Discourse on Method* (New York: Barnes and Noble Publishing, Inc., 2004), 82.

2. Ibid., 130.

3. Peter Hanns Refil and Ellen Judy Wilson, *Encyclopedia of the Enlightenment* (New York: Book Builders Inc., 1996), 206.

4. C.A. Anderson Scott, *Christianity According to St. Paul* (London, N.W: Cambridge University Press, 1961), 99.

CHAPTER THREE

Thinking Affects Your Talking and Walking

EXPRESS YOURSELF

We learned in Chapter One that the Hebrew word for "mind" is *nephesh*, which refers to the inner mind. And in addition to the inner mind, there is also an outer part of the mind. This outer part of the mind is *peh* from the etymological root word *paah*, that is, the mouth. The Bible says, *"...For the mouth speaks out of that which fills the heart"* (Matt. 12:34). The mouth is the expression of the outer side of the mind, which is the external manifestation of one's character and disposition. In essence, the mouth is the organ through which one's relationship with God is ascertained. God said, *"Believe in your heart"*—yes, and then—*"confess with your mouth [peh]"* because the mouth speaks.

The chief way that God has designed man to express himself is through speech. Speech is generated as you exhale the breath that is within you, and the breath is given shape as it passes over your vocal cords."[1]

You speak or express praise from the *peh* or outer part of the mind. However, before you can praise God, you must have a mind to praise Him. And when you set your mind on praising God, you set your life on it, your person on it; you set your whole being on it. When God sets His mind on something, He sets His mind on it through *your* mind.

And when God's Spirit blows His thoughts into your mind, then the will of God must come to pass. When the Spirit of Christ moves in your life, you will no longer be manipulated through your flesh.

The thoughts of the mind are usually expressed through the words of the mouth; thus, anytime there is an expression through the mouth, there is first a thought in the spirit. Consequently, it is logical that expressive people are thinking people, and if you are not thinking, you have nothing to express. We can then assume that God talks much because He thinks much. And because God has so much to tell us, He blows His thoughts into our bodies to make us living thoughts. But even though God's thoughts are formed in man's spirit, neither the character nor the thoughts of a man are evident until they are given expression from the man.

Descartes theorized in *Meditation III* that it is from God's breath that you get your ideas. Descartes believed that God caused the idea of God in his mind. As a result of his belief, he then inquired into the subject of how he received this idea from God. He came to the conclusion that this idea is innate in him; because from the moment of his creation, God imposed the idea of Himself in the mind of Descartes very much like a worker stamping his name to the product of his making.

Descartes further hypothesized that he apprehended this idea in the same intuitive way that he understood the fact of his own thinking existence. Interestingly, He did not deduce God's existence because he knew this immediately and intuitively. Descartes then concluded, "The contemplation of the idea of God is the source of greatest happiness in life. Although he admits that this is incomparably less perfect than the contemplation of God in the life to come as faith suggests, it is a fact of experience that the contemplation of God provides great happiness."[2]

In comparison to what Descartes said, God is saying, "When I blow My Spirit into you, I AM going to release you from your flesh, because your flesh will kill your vision." When we are connected to God, we can reach into the Spirit and speak the Word to break the power of the enemy all around us.

WORDS ARE THOUGHTS OF THE HEART

The Bible says, *"For as he thinks within himself, so he is"* (Prov. 23:7). The Hebrew concept of "heart" is the word *leb*. When the word *leb* is used in the Bible, every immaterial function of a man is attributed to his heart: *"As a man thinks in his heart, so is he."* This refers not to his face, nor to his physicality, but to what is happening on the inside of him—in his mind.

The heart, *leb*, then becomes the biblical term for the totality of man's inner or immaterial nature. In biblical literature, it is believed to be the most frequently used term for man's immaterial personality function as well as the most inclusive term.

Blaise Pascal (1623-1662), a French mathematician, physicist, and religious philosopher, advocated a religious doctrine that taught the experience of God through the heart rather than through reason.[3] So the heart has its own logic and its own reasons, which may be different from those reasons derived from the senses, but they are just as valid, because our inner most thoughts come from the heart. In essence, words are the voice of the heart.

WALK ACCORDING TO THE SPIRIT AND LIVE

Another Hebrew word, *ruah*, means "wind or breath that is spacious." *Ruah* in the Old Testament is translated into the Greek word *pneuma*, and it means "air in motion"—the Holy Spirit. Considering the Day of Pentecost, the Bible says, *"When the day of Pentecost had come, they were all together in one place. And suddenly there came from heaven a noise like a violent rushing wind, and it filled the whole house where they were sitting. And there appeared to them tongues as of fire distributing themselves, and they rested on each one of them. And they were all filled with the Holy Spirit and began to speak with other tongues, as the Spirit was giving them utterance"* (Acts 2:1-4).

In order to understand the relationship between spirit and breath, it is imperative that you understand the relationship of the Father, the Son (Word), and the Holy Spirit (wind in motion). It's the Spirit of God who blows into your nostrils, who refreshes and brings new life to your mind. Thus, to maintain control of your mind, you have to be connected to the Holy Spirit of God. The Holy Spirit is the key; and the law of the Spirit—not a written law—is the regulated principle of the Holy Spirit.

The law of the Spirit, or in other words, the regulative principle of the Holy Spirit, which exercises control over the life of the believer, provides energy from the Spirit that gives you a desire to come out of where you are and go where the Lord wants you to go. This energy comes from the Spirit of God and blows naturally into your mind. As the Lord blows His Spirit into you, the energy from His Spirit will take you higher into the next level. The Lord will blow into your spirit until you can tell the world and satan that:

◆ I am coming out; I can't stay in the box.

◆ I have to come out. I am tired of being restricted, held back.

◆ I am coming out of poverty, depression, and low self-esteem.

◆ I am out of the box.

◆ I will never be the same because I am moving in the power of my anointing.

◆ I am liberated.

◆ I am free.

◆ No weapon formed against me shall prosper.

You are now empowered to defeat satan and to walk according to the Spirit because the Spirit who raised Jesus from the dead is the same Spirit who is alive in each of us. Consequently, we are no longer restricted by the carnal mind; we are no longer under law but are now under grace; we don't owe the flesh any favors at all, we are debtors to the Holy Spirit because Jesus conquered the grave to purchase our redemption; Christ Jesus did it by the power of the Holy Spirit. That same Spirit is now available to you. Thus, you have an obligation to live according to the Spirit because you are now spiritually minded, and *"There is therefore now no condemnation to those who are in Christ Jesus"* (Romans 8:1)

ENDNOTES

1. John Herrin, "Yahweh, His Breath and His Word" Heart 4 God, 18 June 2003, accessed 3 December 2005; available from http://heart4god.8k.com.

2. René Descartes, *Discourse on Method*, 108.

3. Blaise Pascal, *Pensees* (London, England: Penguin Group, translated 1995), 28.

CHAPTER FOUR

Freeing Yourself From the Box

The apostle Paul boldly declares to all believers, *"There is therefore now no condemnation to those who are in Christ Jesus..."* (Rom. 8:1). To you who are in Christ Jesus, God has breathed His Spirit into your soul—your mind (*nephesh*); and because your mind is connected to the Spirit of God, you are therefore released to God's original intention for your life.

Consequently, your mind wants to be at home with the Spirit of God. It's like—"E.T., go home." You may recall the popular movie, *E.T.*, which was released in 1982. At one point in the movie, E.T. (an alien from another planet) had nothing else on his mind but to go home. He had a very interesting and enjoyable experience while visiting Earth; he was treated very well and was taken care of. But even though E.T. was living with a loving family and was adored by the children, he still was an alien away from his original home. The planet Earth was not E.T.'s original habitat, and even after having so much fun, he wanted to go back home to his own environment.

Just like E.T., you might be saying, "I know the world is all right and there are some good things here, but there is something greater— my home. I am not currently able to do all of the things I am capable of, but I want to reach my full potential. I want to be released from this box of sinful flesh so that I can be all that God has called me to be, and achieve everything that God has placed in my mind."

I Am Free—The Flesh No Longer Holds Me

Because you are now "in Christ Jesus," no matter what environment you are placed in or where you may stay for a while, you will find that the flesh is never good enough. It is too restricting; your thoughts and your will have now been elevated beyond your situations. When you look at God's original intention for your life, you'll understand that your mind wants intimacy with God, without the restriction of your flesh or your environment. Consequently, you will not be satisfied until you are released from the box of sinful flesh and your mind is connected to the Spirit of Christ.

With your spirit connected to the Spirit of Christ, you can now focus with a single mind that is "in Christ Jesus." And with this single mind in Christ Jesus, you can do whatever God has created you to do. Flesh creatures will not be able to distract you. Therefore, as soon as you begin to feel that releasing power of God, you can rise up out of your box of flesh and declare, "I shall have everything that is mine. I shall have what God said I can have." You can boldly make this declaration because the Bible says, *"But if the Spirit of Him who raised Jesus from the dead dwells in you, He who raised Christ Jesus from the dead will also give life to your mortal bodies through His Spirit who dwells in you"* (Rom. 8:11).

In order to release yourself from condemnation, however, you have to know that the Spirit of God, who raised Jesus from the dead, is the same Spirit that is alive in you. It is significant that you understand this concept because when this thought becomes real in your mind, *you* will know that it is time for *you* to get control of your mind, get rid of the negative imprints, and move to the next level of your walk in the Spirit of Christ.

In addition, because it is in the mind where the real battle is fought, you have to personally maintain power over the flesh. At the same time, you must be aware that while it is not easy to conquer the power of the flesh overnight, every believer has the ability, by connecting to the Spirit of God through the Word of God, to receive power over the flesh in order to win the battle in the mind. Moreover, when you are in Christ and have been released into the power of God, then you can walk in His Spirit because you are:

- ◆ Free to rise up above your circumstances.
- ◆ Free to be a powerhouse in the middle of a dying world.
- ◆ Free to speak things as they are and bring them to pass.
- ◆ Free to express yourself in a world of contradictions.
- ◆ Free to look up and declare, "The devil thought he had me, but God has set me free."

REDEMPTION—THE PRICE HAS BEEN PAID

Now the questions become:

1. "How can I believe that the Lord can take me to the next level if I don't believe that I can go there myself?" and

2. "How can I believe that the Lord has forgiven me if I don't forgive myself?"

Both these questions bring us back to the act of faith, and your action becomes the evidence of your faith. When you take a look at condemnation, you will find that it causes you to process negative thoughts about yourself, and when these thoughts are locked into your mind, you will not release yourself to the power that you have in Christ Jesus. It is also true that we are in the habit of thinking that we have to work things out for ourselves because we have this inherent nature as sinful man to want to toil and to work; it is our punishment for Adam's sin. But it is through the Word that the Spirit of Christ releases all believers from bondage, while the flesh is fighting with the spirit.

As sinful man we innately want to work out every situation as we try to solve our every problem on our own, which is contradistinctive to the cry of the spirit man. Moreover, the concept of "let go and let God" has been intellectualized and thereby diminishes its spiritual impact to release ourselves to the power that we have in Christ Jesus.

The fact is, we are now free, and because of Jesus' death and resurrection we are entitled to complete justification, substitution, and sanctification. As we look at the Lord's design of man, we learn a great truth about the Father, Son, and Spirit. The spirit of man is invisible, but it is his spirit that determines who he is; essentially, your character is bound up in your spirit, and the Spirit of Christ wants to communicate with your spirit—your mind. Christ has redeemed us from the law of sin and death to the law of the Spirit of life in Christ. The primary condition of Christ's work in redemption is the incarnation of Christ Jesus who knew no sin, but was sent in the likeness of sinful flesh to die for mankind. He gave His life as the substitution for what the Law could not do, weak as it was through the flesh. God sent His own Son in the "likeness of sinful flesh" and as an offering for sin. We must therefore always emphasize that while the Son of God came "in flesh," He did not come in "flesh of sin" but in the "likeness of sinful flesh" (Rom. 8:3).

REUNITED WITH GOD

The mind longs to reunite with God, and we have to think through our circumstances as we think ourselves out of the bondage of our situations. Where the Spirit (*nephesh*) of the Lord is, there is liberty; and the mind (*nephesh*) longs to be free from being a slave to the flesh.

You have to now say, "Get the shackles off me. I am getting ready to break out because I am a child of God." You are coming out of the box of your sinful flesh and removing the shackles of your mind. You are coming out of the box because you want to know the will of God for your own life. You are coming out of the box, and you don't want limits or parameters set around your mind. You are an original; and you cannot be duplicated, cannot be imitated, and cannot be destroyed. You can therefore walk in the world but not be governed by the environment and standards of the world. You have been created by God. The world can scrape through all the façade and look at the beautiful, powerful, joyful you—God's original and new creation.

CHAPTER FIVE

Theological and Philosophical Thoughts and Concepts

THE MIND IS THE SEAT OF ALL SPIRITUAL AND CARNAL EXPRESSIONS

THEOLOGY	PHILOSOPHY
Theological View—Body and Soul	Philosophical Concept—Dualism
A traditional Christian's view is that the mind is a distinct reality. You have a soul, which is different from your body; your body will die and then your soul will go to Heaven or hell. The historical record of God's formation of man provides the key to an understanding of the essential nature of man. Genesis 2:7—*"And the Lord God formed man of dust from the ground, and breathed into his nostrils the breath of life; and man became a living being."*	In philosophy of mind, dualism is a set of beliefs that begin with the claim that mental events and physical events are totally different kinds of events.[1] Issues and concerns of the "mind-body" dates back at least to Plato, who was considered the first dualist. Plato contends that the soul is distinct from the body and is capable of maintaining a separate existence from it. (Assumes the mind and body are two separate and distinct parts—material and immaterial).[2] According to Descartes, God created two classes of substances that make up the whole of reality: thinking substances (minds) and extended substances (bodies).[3]

Other Scriptural references:

Romans 7:23-25—*"but I see a different law in the members of my body, waging war against the law of my mind and making me a prisoner of the law of sin which is in my members. Wretched man that I am! Who will set me free from the body of this death? Thanks be to God through Jesus Christ our Lord! So then, on the one hand I myself with my mind am serving the law of God, but on the other, with my flesh the law of sin."*

In relating his own personal experience as a Christian, Paul declares that he is carnal, a creature of the flesh, sold under sin, in captivity to sin; consequently, the indwelling depravity of human nature rebels against God's law. The good news is that because we have the law of the Spirit of life, we have the victory over the law of sin in the flesh.

Psalm 63:1—*"O God, You are my God; I shall seek You earnestly; My soul thirsts for You, my flesh yearns for You, In a dry and weary land where there is no water."*

Ecclesiastes 12:7—*"Then the dust will return to the earth as it was, and the spirit will return to God who gave it."*

Matthew 10:28—*"Do not fear those who kill the body but are unable to kill the soul. But rather fear Him who is able to destroy both soul and body in hell."*

Romans 8:10—*"And if Christ is in you, the body is dead because of sin, yet the Spirit is alive because of righteousness."*

Descartes—"And although we suppose that God united a body to a soul so closely that it was impossible to form a more intimate union, and thus made a composite whole, the two substances would remain really distinct, notwithstanding this union."[4]

Philo said that in the early ages a sharp distinction was made between the principles of good and evil. He thought that the spiritual part of man, his mind or soul, is the seat of good, and his body, the material part, is the seat of evil. Consequently, when the soul is incorporated in the body it suffers a fall from divine perfection and becomes predisposed to evil. Thus, the goal of man is freedom from matter and a return to God who is perfect goodness.[5]

Descartes—"If you would be a real seeker of truth, it is necessary that at least once in your life you doubt, as far as possible, all things."[6]

Saint Augustine—On the Immortality of the Soul, he said, "But the soul is present as a whole not only in the entire mass of a body, but also in every least part of the body at the same time."[7]

John Calvin—French theologian and leader of Calvinism, "Seeing that a pilot steers the ship in which we sail, who will never allow to perish even in the midst of shipwrecks, there is no reason why our minds should be overwhelmed with fear and overcome with weariness."[8]

Romans 12:1-2—*"Therefore I urge you, brethren, by the mercies of God, to present your bodies a living and holy sacrifice, acceptable to God, which is your spiritual service of worship. And do not be conformed to this world, but be transformed by the renewing of your mind, so that you may prove what the will of God is, that which is good and acceptable and perfect."*

First Corinthians 5:5—*"Deliver such a one to satan for the destruction of his flesh, that his spirit may be saved in the day of Lord Jesus."*

Colossians 2:5—*"For though I am absent in the flesh, yet I am with you in spirit."*

Galatians 5:17-18—*"For the flesh sets its desire against the Spirit, and the Spirit against the flesh; for these are in opposition to one another, so that you may not do the things that you please. But if you are led by the Spirit, you are not under the law."* Paul is reminding us that because we are in Christ, we have control over sin in the flesh. Thus, when the flesh sets its desire against the Spirit, the law of the Spirit in Christ overrules the law of sin and death. Hence, we can win the battle of sin in the flesh in the mind.

Galatians 5:24-25—*now those who belong to Christ Jesus have crucified the flesh with its passions and desires. If we live by the Spirit, let us also walk by the Spirit."* He is declaring that when the Holy Spirit indwells us and we walk according to the Spirit, we have the power of the Holy Spirit to have victory over satan.

Saint Augustine—"My mind withdrew its thoughts from experience, extracting itself from the contradictory throng of sensuous images, that it might find out what that light was wherein it was bathed....And thus, with the flash of one hurried glance, it attained to the vision of That Which Is."[9]

Thomas Aquinas (an early Christian thinker)—"To achieve goodness is the highest good, and the greatest good for man is to realize God's purpose in the creation of man. The best way to attain goodness is to abandon worldly things and seek communion with God.... Evil is the absence of good and when an object fails to achieve good results, evil comes into being."[10]

Descartes—When asked, "How is it possible for an immaterial substance to come into contact with a material substance?" Descartes simply stated that he "inhabits his body like a pilot in a vessel; and that the body is strictly a mechanical and machine-like substance. Its functions are entirely different from those of the spirit. The spirit is synonymous with mind.... The mind serves as the director of the body."[11]

Blaise Pascal—"The immorality of the soul is something of such vital importance to us, affecting us so deeply, that one must have lost all feeling not to care about knowing the facts of the matter."[12]

J. Gresham Machen—"I think we ought to hold not only that man has a soul, but that it is important that he should know that he has a soul."[13]

Ephesians 5:15-18—*"Therefore be careful how you walk, not as unwise men but as wise, making the most of your time, because the days are evil. So then do not be foolish, but understand what the will of the Lord is. And do not get drunk with wine, for that is dissipation, but be filled with the Spirit."*	Descartes—In the Fourth Meditation, Descartes proclaimed, "If I always saw clearly what was true and good, I should never have to deliberate about the right judgement or choice." He also asserts that his belief in extra-mental reality cannot be due to any deceptive action of God. God is a perfect being and deception is imperfect by its nature. Any mental errors that exist in his mind find their sources in his imperfect nature.[14] According to Aristotle, "Moral weakness of the will results in someone doing what is wrong, knowing that it is right, and yet follows his desire against reason." For Aristotle, this condition is not a myth; the problem is a matter of conflicting moral principles.[15]

ENDNOTES

1. René Descartes, *Discourse on Method*, 130.

2. J.P. Moreland and William Lane Craig, *Philosophical Foundations for a Christian Worldview* (Madison, WI: InterVasity Press, 2003), 507.

3. René Descartes, *Discourse on Method*, 130.

4. Ibid.

5. Chase B. Wrenn "Philo of Alexandria," Internet Encyclopedia of Philosophy, accessed 1 February 2005; available from: http:www.iep.utm.edu/research/iep/philo.htm.

6. René Descartes, *Discourse on Method*, 9.

7. Saint Augustine, *The Confessions of Saint Augustine*, accessed 3 March 2005; available from: http://www.mb.soft.com/believer/txn/august.htm.

8. John Calvin, translated by Henry Beveridge, *Institutes of the Christian Religion* (Grand Rapids, MI: Wm. B. Eerdmans Publishing, 2006).

9. Saint Augustine, *The Confessions of Saint Augustine,* accessed 3 March 2005; available from: http://www.mb.soft.com/believer/txn/august.htm.

10. Ralph McInerny and John O'Callaghan "Saint Thomas Aquinas," *The Standard Encyclopedia of Philosophy* (Spring 2005 Edition), Edward N. Zalta (ed.), accessed 13 September 2005; available from:http://plato.standard.edu/archives/spr2005/entries/aquinas/.

11. René Descartes, *Discourse on Method.*

12. Blaise Pascal, *Pensees* (London, England: Penguin Group), 128.

13. J. Gresham Machen, "God the Creator" *The Christian Faith in the Modern World,* (Grand Rapids MI:Wm. B. Eerdmans Publishing, 1993), accessed 3 June 2005; available from http://www.christianbeliefs.org/books/ChrFaith-Machen-00.htm.

14. René Descartes, *Discourse on Method.*

15. Aristotle, *On The Soul,* cited by Chase B. Wrenn, *Internet Encyclopedia of Philosophy,* February 2005, accessed 25 August 2005; available from http://www.iep.utm.edu/.

Meanings and Explanations With Use and Application

CARNAL (GK: *SARX*\SARX)

STRONG #4563: flesh (as stripped of the skin), i.e. bodily temporal, or animal, unregenerate: the body (as opposed to the soul {or spirit}, human nature with its frailties and passions).

VINE: From sarx, "flesh," signifies "having the nature of flesh," i.e. sensual, controlled by animal appetites, governed by human nature, instead of by the Spirit of God. It is as the equivalent of "human," with the added idea of weakness, figuratively of the weapons of spiritual warfare, of the flesh" or with the idea of unspirituality, of human wisdom, "fleshly," as in Second Corinthians 1:12; and "retaining to the flesh" (i.e., the body) as in Romans 15:27.

WEBSTER: relating to or given to crude bodily pleasures and appetites; marked by sexuality; bodily, corporeal, temporal and worldly. The physical nature of human beings.

USE AND APPLICATION: Be clear that any hostile or disobedient tendency toward God's Word comes out of carnal (fleshly) nature.

CONDEMNATION (GK: *KATAKRIMA*\KAT-AK-REE-MAH)

STRONG #2631: an adverse sentence (the verdict) to judge against.

VINE: (cf. 2632), to give judgment against, pass sentence upon; to condemn," implying (a) the fact of a crime; (b) the imputation of a crime, as in the "condemnation" of Christ by the Jews.

WEBSTER: Censure, blame; the act of judicially condemning; the state of being condemned.

USE AND APPLICATION: Understand that no matter how you may feel, Christ Jesus will not condemn you because you belong to Him. Jesus said, *"Truly, truly, I say to you, he who hears My Word, and believes Him who sent Me, has eternal life, and does not come into judgment, but has passed out of death into life."* (John 5:24).

LAW (GK: *NOMOS*\NOM OS)

STRONG #3551: through the idea of prescriptive usage, (regulation), spec. (of Moses; also of the Gospel), or figuratively a (principle): law.

VINE: To divide out, distribute, primarily meant "that which is assigned"; "usage, custom," as <u>decreed by a state and set up as the standard for administration of justice.</u>

WEBSTER: A binding custom or practice of a community; a rule of conduct or action prescribed or formally recognized as binding or enforced by a controlling authority.

USE AND APPLICATION: The law here does not refer to God's written moral commands in the Old Testament, but to the system of operation that the Spirit of life, the Holy Spirit, carries them out in our lives, breaking the dominion of the old law (principle) of sin and death. (Ref. Spirit-filled Bible commentary notes.)

MIND (GK: *PHRONEO*)

STRONG #5426: to exercise the mind, i.e. entertain or have a sentiment or opinion; by implication to be (mentally) disposed (more or less earnestly in a certain direction) from. *"phren"* (#5424) to interest oneself in (with concern or obedience): set the affection on, (be) careful, be like, be of one, be of the same, let this mind (ed, regard, savior, think).

VINE: "To think, to be minded in a certain way"; (b) "to think of, be mindful of." It implies moral interest or reflection, not mere unreasoning opinion. In Romans 8:5, *"For those who are according to the flesh set their minds on the things of the flesh"*; literally means "minding the same," and "set (not) your mind on," things of the flesh.

USE AND APPLICATION: When the mind is renewed by the Holy Spirit, the whole mind is set to have understanding, be wise; to feel, to think to have an opinion of one's self, think of one's self, to be modest, not let one's opinion (though just) of himself exceed the bounds of modesty; to think or judge what one's opinion is; to be of the same mind, i.e., agreed together, cherish the same views, be harmonious; to direct one's mind to a thing, and to seek, to strive for.

MIND (GK. *PHRONEMA*\FRON—AY-MAH)

STRONG #5427: From *phroneo* (#2426); (mental) inclination or purpose: (be, be carnally, be spiritually) mind.

VINE: Denotes "what one has in the mind, the thought" (the content of the process expressed in phroneo, "to have in mind, to think"); or "an object of thought."

USE AND APPLICATION: What one has in the mind, the thoughts and purposes. The verb behind set their minds, refers to the basic orientation, bent, and thought patterns of the mind, rather than to the mind or intellect itself (Greek *nous*). It includes a person's affections and will, as well as his reasoning. Paul uses the same verb in Philippians, where he admonishes believers to *"have this attitude* [mind] *in you which was also in Christ Jesus."* (Phil. 2:5)

Practical Applications

There is a struggle to walk in the promises of God because there is a constant battle for control of the mind. When we accept Christ Jesus into our lives as Lord and Savior, there is an internal struggle between two forces—the law of sin and death and the law of the Spirit of life. In essence, accepting Jesus actually introduces you to internal conflict because the carnal mind (the mind of the flesh) sets its desires against the mind of the Spirit. So walking with God is not conflict free because there is a constant battle for control of the mind.

It is important that you think of some specific applications and reflections to apply both the theological and philosophical lessons learned to correctly understand:

- The mind is the seat of carnal and spiritual expressions; and you are to walk according to the Spirit.

- *"There is therefore now no condemnation,"* (Romans 8:1) means Jesus not only paid the debt of sin but also cleansed us *"from all unrighteousness"* (I John 1:9).

Even though Christian believers are no longer under the dominion of sin, we will always experience conflicts with sin in this present life.

However, we have the promise that although we still stumble and fall into sin's power in our flesh, we will experience ultimate victory over sin.

ACTION STEPS

Actions to take or things to do in order to apply faith to defeat satan and to walk according to the Spirit:

A. Seek God with all your heart and with all your soul.

1. Begin by praising God for what He has already done.

2. Meditate on what God is saying in the Scripture (read Romans 8:1-13) and ask the Holy Spirit to lead you in prayer for guidance and understanding of God's Word.

3. Ask God for what you want. With prayer and supplication let your request be known. Ask the Holy Spirit to reveal God's truth and the will of God for you.

4. Worship God in Spirit and in Truth, and commit yourself to being transformed by the Word.

5. Make a commitment to spend at least 30 minutes a day with *God only*.

6. Make a commitment to fast and pray at least one day each week.

7. Pray and praise God again—just give Him thanks and praise.

B. Begin each day in the reality that you are a new creature and that the Spirit of Christ dwells in you, and you are no longer under condemnation for past sins.

C. Pray inwardly for the Lord to open your mind and understanding so you can learn the practical characteristics of a mind that is walking according to the Spirit and not according to the flesh.

D. Spend time reading and studying God's Word.

1. Prayerfully and carefully read John 14:17 to understand that the mind that is directed toward truth is aware that

the Spirit of Christ dwells (lives) in you, and that you are to be aware that you are always in His presence.

2. Read Romans 6:8 to understand how to please God by sowing seeds for the harvest.

3. Sow the Word in order to win souls by sharing the Gospel and telling others of God's love, grace, and mercy. Note: living evangelistically is not only a privilege; it is rewarding. The following Scriptures are valuable tools for guiding others to salvation: John 3:16; Romans 10:9-10; and Acts 4:12.

PERSONAL GROWTH AND DEVELOPMENT

The most important thing that you can do to walk according to the Spirit is to read and study the Word daily. Walking according to the Spirit and being controlled by the Spirit of Christ does not happen through osmosis; it comes by being obedient to His Word. That is by studying and applying the Scripture until it is written on your heart and in your mind.

The following Scriptures are valuable tools for understanding that *love* fulfills the law when you are walking according to the Spirit: Romans 15:14; First Corinthians 13:7-8; Galatians 5:16-26; Colossians 3:12-16; John 15:2.

Pray and ask the Holy Spirit to lead you in prayer for guidance, repentance, and thanksgiving.

One way to guide your prayer is to remember the acronym ACTS:

A= Adoration for honor for God.

C = Confession of your sins.

T = Thanksgiving and praise for what God has done.

S = Supplication/Intercession (praying for the needs of others).

READ, RECORD, REFLECT

To gain more from your time in the Scripture, you should read and reread the passage.

You must know what the passage says before you can understand what it means and how it applies to you and your ministry. You should:

- ◆ Read to determine, "What does this passage say to me?" Begin by reading the passage to determine what the Scripture is all about.

- ◆ Record what you see. It is extremely important that you write some notes and keep a record of your insights and questions.

- ◆ Mark unfamiliar words or phrases that you do not understand; and write your answers in your journal or study notes.

PART TWO

Finding Your Original Self

Who am I? That is the question all of us ask ourselves. It is easy to get lost in the busyness of life so that in the end it is our activity that defines who we are. That's why so many people become addicted to their work. They are seeking to establish their identity from what they do instead of who they are. Whether you are a businessperson or a stay-at-home mom, it is easy to allow your identity to be defined by what you do.

Jesus came to establish the uniqueness of who we are, not based upon works, but upon creation. In His inaugural message, Jesus reversed the natural order of perceptions, making it clear that what is inside a person determines the man or woman, not what they appear to be on the outside. In this section, we will help you refocus, and end the masquerade, so you can discover your original self.

CHAPTER SIX

I Am an Original

A ONE AND ONLY

There is no one like me in the whole wide world; no one has my DNA, my fingerprints, or my voice print. As we consider what it means to be an original, we turn our attention to apostle Paul's appeal for renewing the mind found in Romans chapter 12:

> *"Therefore I urge you, brethren, by the mercies of God, to present your bodies a living and holy sacrifice, acceptable to God, which is your spiritual service of worship. And do not be conformed to this world, but be transformed by the renewing of your mind, so that you may prove what the will of God is, that which is good and acceptable and perfect"* (Romans 12:1-2).

These verses introduce the transition from the theological presentation of the Gospel to what is called exaltation; and that is to move us from those things that God has done for us into how we should respond. So it is in the beginning of Romans chapter 12 that Paul urges us to measure our lives to our belief.

CONNECTED TO LIFE, OR DISCONNECTED AND DYING

We will compare and contrast the differences between a conformed mind (to copy) and a transformed mind (to create). Interestingly, the comparison can be illustrated by the remarkable differences between water in a pond and the water in a river. The water in a river constantly moves and flows while water in a pond is stagnated or stilled. A river is connected to other bodies of water; thus water moves in and out. This continuous movement indicates that changes are constantly taking place, or that the water is living.

A pond, on the other hand, is a detached body of water; it stands alone. Because there is no continuous flow of water entering or leaving the pond, the water in it is often stagnated; and when water is stilled and stagnated, it stinks with dead and decaying matter.

As we further ponder the analogy of a river and pond, we can compare it to ourselves being connected to a life source—the Spirit of Christ, which flows through a person's faith—his belief in Christ Jesus, into his spirit. However, if the person is not connected to the life source, then the mind is not being refreshed and renewed. And when the mind is not being refreshed, it becomes stale and causes one to act or react in ways that are not symbolic of who he really is.

When your life is stale, there is no creativity because your mind is stilled and stagnated. Nothing happens in a stale life but more depression. It is significant then to understand the mind from the Hebrew concept of *nephesh* mentioned earlier, which regards the mind as being life, soul, creature, person, and appetite. The original or etymological root of the Hebrew word *nephesh* is to breathe, to refresh oneself. The mind becomes the very core of the individual; it's your inner self, your heart, and your person—it's you.

The Hebrew term for "spirit"—*ruah,* is a metaphorical term to describe an activity or vitality; it has the same meaning as the Greek term, *pneuma,* which means wind or breath. According to Scripture, the ruah, *pneuma,* or the Holy Spirit is the "the physical breath of life" (see Gen. 2:7; 6:17; 7:15).

Because you are now connected to the Spirit of Christ, the Living Water, your mind is being renewed and refreshed with the original and creative breath or wind from the Holy Spirit of God. Essentially, God's Spirit (breath) is flowing into your spirit; and consequently, you are constantly being transformed by the renewing of the mind to be more and more like Christ Jesus. Thus, we are now called to live a different lifestyle than what the world offers. We are not to conform to the world's values of selfishness, corruption, unethical behavior, and customs.

It is critical for us to understand that there has to be a personal connection to the life source—the Holy Spirit (*ruah* or *pneuma*)—the "breath" or "wind" of life—flowing through faith into your spirit, and then into your mind, which is symbolic of who you are. The mind then becomes the very essence of who you are. Thus, every one of us can say, "My mind is my inner self; it's my heart; it's my soul; it's my appetite; it's my total person; it's who I am."

It is in the mind where the Spirit of God transforms or spawns creativity. Creativity does not take place from outside the mind; rather, we create from an inner personal connection to the very breath of God. Therefore, when we are not connected to the Living Water, our lives become stale as stilled water in a stagnated pond. And when your life is stale, there is no creativity; nothing happens when life is stale or dying.

As long as we are living, our bodies are always generating new cells. No matter how old a person is, his body is constantly renewing itself because renewal is a part of the life process. On the other hand, anyone who is not renewing is dead, and dead things are completely controlled by the environment. Dead people cannot tell you what to do with their bodies; they cannot argue, neither can they resist.

Likewise, an individual who no longer has the strength to stand on his own connection to his life source then seeks to find strength in conforming (being like everybody else). Whenever one lives according to the dictates of others, he cannot connect to the will of God for his own life. Therefore he has a greater propensity to become more of a copy than an original.

We must always be mindful that the world desires to conform and wants to be like someone else; so much so, that most of us don't even know who we are because we have not tapped into the Source of life that flows as Living water, which is renewing and refreshing. This constant flow from the life source refreshes our mind and prevents us from conforming, thus allowing us to be creative. When we are connected to the life source, we no longer live our lives the way the world wants us to live. We now live the way God intends us to live.

THE LIVING WATER

It is significant to understand the concept that Christ Jesus projects when He declares, "...*If anyone is thirsty, let him come to Me and drink."He who be-lieves in Me, as the Scripture said, 'From his innermost being will flow rivers of living water.'*" (John 7:37-38). Jesus is saying that it doesn't matter what your environment is; it doesn't matter what's going on around you. Because if you are connected to Him, then everything that has bogged you down and stalemated you is now flowing out of you because He is pouring His life back into you.

Understanding that Christ is the flowing river of Living Water can be compared to water being central to Israel's whole economy and existence. During biblical times, the rabbis taught the principles of water and rain. Water was a very important part of the Feast of Tabernacles and the holy days of Sukkot. (It was during this festival time that Jesus Christ said, *"If anyone is thirsty, let him come to Me and drink"* [John 7:37].)

By way of illustration, the priest would pour the water over the altar to signify Israel's gratitude for the rain that had produced the harvest and would pray for rain in the coming months. The priest would recite a hymn of praise:

> *"Then you will say on that day, 'I will give thanks to You, O LORD; For although You were angry with me, Your anger is turned away, And You comfort me. Behold, God is my salvation, I will trust and not be afraid; For the LORD GOD is my strength and song, And He has be-come my salvation.'Therefore you will joyously draw water From the springs of salvation."* (Isaiah 12:1-3).

And so, in exchange for our bodies as a living sacrifice, the Spirit of the Lord is saying to each of us, "I am pouring life back into you." And as God's Spirit flows through your mind, He is transforming you into a new creature. You are now one of God's original creations. You have a renewed mind.

It is important to understand that because God renews from the inside, He prevents us from adapting to the circumstances and situations that could affect us from the outside. It is this new life source flowing through our mind that strengthens us to become defiant in the face of adversity. We are enabled to stand no matter how great the environmental influences because He has delivered us from being dead in sin. God wants a living sacrifice, not a dead one.

CHAPTER SEVEN

How to Change Yourself

Have you felt trapped in a situation, somewhere you did not want to be, then all of a sudden you broke free by the power of your own intuition, by the power of your connection with God? If so, then you understand that there is nothing more refreshing than being liberated, delivered, and set free from a relationship or being tied to someone who has been controlling your mind and maintaining dominion over you.

There is nothing more liberating than standing on your own two feet with your security in your faith in God, knowing that the Spirit of Christ is flowing through you. He has liberated you from conforming to the sinful desires of a carnal mind so that satan and his demons no longer have dominion over your mind. And as God is flowing through you, He wants to glorify Himself in you.

Now that you are transformed and have a new mind, you can dictate to your environment. God has created you to have dominion over your environment. However, God wants each one of us to have control over self before having dominion over the environment.

It is quite important to note that while God created you to have dominion over the environment, He did not create you to have control over me, nor did He create me to have control over you. In fact, one writer said, "God the creator never intended man to rule over or dominate his own, but rather to rule the creation and resources of earth."[1]

CHANGED FROM THE INSIDE

We have been transformed by the renewing of our mind, and God's Spirit (breath) is flowing into our spirit so that we can maintain control over our carnal and sinful desires of the flesh so that our mind can become more and more like Christ Jesus. In order for transformation to take place, however, a *change* must occur. The word *change* has a variety of meanings; some dictionary definitions of change include: to become different or undergo alternation; to undergo transformation or transition; to go from one phase to another to make different in form; to transform, to give and take reciprocally; to become different.

Early philosophers objected to the notion of *change* being real because they believed that "something that is, cannot come to be"; and since they believed that something cannot come from nothing, they maintained that change is impossible. Aristotle, on the other hand, discarded this concept by introducing the notions of defining *change* in a thing as "the passage from potentiality to actuality." Aristotle used this concept in physics to explain potential energy (energy at rest, dead, and not moving) and kinetic energy (energy in motion, alive, flowing, and changing).[2]

When applying Aristotle's concept of change to transforming the mind, we can say that during the process of being transformed by the renewing of our mind, a *change* occurs. Our mind changes from carnal to spirit. However, the renewal and *change* can take place only because we are connected to the source of power—the Living Water—the Spirit of Christ.

To change from potentiality (wanting to be in Christ) to actuality (being in Christ), there must be an external force (the Holy Spirit) or pressure applied for you to realize your ability to change from the state of potential to one of actual being. The Spirit of Christ is the power that transforms, changes, and moves us from potentiality (being conformed) to actuality (being transformed) by the renewing of our minds.

Change can be temporary; examples include going on vacation for two weeks, rearranging the furniture, changing the color of your hair, or going on a diet and losing 20 pounds. Change can also be long term or permanent. Once your birthday comes, you will never go back to a younger age. When one reaches the age of 21, you can never go back to age 19 or 20. A permanent or eternal change is making a commitment to Christ as Lord and Savior. So being transformed by the renewing of the mind is a permanent change and a commitment to being personally connected to the Spirit of Christ in order to walk according to the Spirit.

John Wesley described the change that God worked in his heart through his faith in Christ: "I felt my heart strangely warmed. I felt I did trust in Christ, Christ alone for salvation, and an assurance was given me that He had taken away my sins, even mind, and saved me from the law of sin and death."[3]

When you have a personal connection to the Holy Spirit of God, He constantly transforms and renews you, taking you from being a potential child of God and changing you into an actual child of God. In essence, you are now renewed and transformed from potentiality (being controlled by the carnal and sinful nature) to actuality (being in Christ and walking according to the will of the Spirit) because Christ Jesus gave His life to release you from the law of sin and death. You are a new and original creation, and everything you have copied from others and incorporated into your mind is now dead or must die.

With your transformed mind you can now expect to win all the battles in your mind because during the transformation process, God blew—and He is still blowing—a winning spirit into your mind. So with the Spirit of Christ connected to your spirit, you can win every mind game that satan tries to play because Holiness now controls your mind—your life, your appetite, and your sexual desires.

GOD IS OUR MATERIAL AND SPIRITUAL SUPPLY

God is now your material and spiritual source of life. Scripture gives us specific incidences when God provided the Israelites with material prosperity that they did not work for. If you consider Deuteronomy

6:10-12, for example, you will find that God had to remind the Is-raelites that they were not to forget:

> *"Then it shall come about when the LORD your God brings you into the land which He swore to your fathers, Abraham, Isaac and Jacob, to give you, great and splendid cities which you did not build, and houses full of all good things which you did not fill, and hewn cisterns which you did not dig, vineyards and olive trees which you did not plant, and you eat and are sat-isfied, then watch yourself, that you do not forget the LORD who brought you from the land of Egypt, out of the house of slavery."* (Deuteronomy 6:10-12).

They were blessed with houses they did not build, food they did not harvest, vineyards and olive trees they did not plant, and water from wells they did not dig. Yet God still had to remind them that they were not to forget their spiritual source of blessing when their physical needs were satisfied. We can see this same principle at work in several other places in Scripture as well as in our lives today.

God supplies our needs in a wilderness where there is nothing. Even in the midst of sickness, poverty, trials, tribulations, and all trou-blesome circumstances and barren surroundings, because when we look to the hills for our help, our *"help comes from the LORD"* (see Ps. 121:2). It is that new life source from the Spirit of Christ that flows through the believers' mind that makes you defiant in the face of adversity. You have the Holy Spirit, and the Bible says, *"For the law of the Spirit of life in Christ Jesus has set you free from the law of sin and death"* (Rom. 8:2).

GOD WANTS A PERSONAL RELATIONSHIP WITH YOU

Yes, you can stand no matter how satan tries to influence your life. You are to live your life the way God intends you to live—according to His perfect will. You no longer want to live according to the desires of the flesh and the dictates of the world. Specifically, when you are able to stand and face the trials and tribulations in your life, then God is saying through His Spirit to your mind:

- ◆ "I like your uniqueness because I created you so I can dwell in you."

- ◆ "I like what I made and I want to move through you."

- ◆ "I want you to come out of the flesh and take your place in My Spirit."

- ◆ "I have had a relationship with somebody like you, but I want to communicate with the real you."

Furthermore, you can continue to stand because Christ Jesus prayed that you would not be removed from the world, but that you be kept from the evil of the world (see John 7:15). You must, therefore, renew yourself constantly, because renewal is a part of the life process; and as long as you are living, your body is generating new cells from the source of life—the Spirit of Christ, which flows as Living Water.

With the Spirit of Christ flowing through your body as Living Water, He establishes an atmosphere in you that has nothing to do with the atmosphere outside; God deals with your mind from the inside. When we consider this concept theologically and philosophically, we know that our relationship with God has to begin within each person. The question then becomes, "Why do I look for God within myself?" The answer: "He indwells my spirit; I talk to God from the inside— spirit to Spirit. His Spirit transforms and renews my mind to be more and more like Christ Jesus. And with the mind of Christ, my mind reveals an attitude of love, joy, peace, longsuffering, kindness, goodness, faithfulness, gentleness, and self-control—that's inside."

We Perceive God by Faith

Clearly, our relationship with God is not just physical, material, or intellectual; our relationship with God is spiritual; and the Spirit is life, and life is mind. Accordingly, John Calvin (1509-64), a prominent advocate of the *five solas* of the Reformation who reorganized organized religion and created a worldwide protestant movement, maintained, "There is within the human mind, and indeed by natural instinct, an awareness of divinity....God himself has implanted in all men a certain understanding of his divine majesty." Closely related to this *sensus divinitatis (sense of divinity)* is an external witness or revelation of God in creation. "Not only," writes Calvin, has God "sowed in men's minds that seed of religion of which we have spoken but revealed himself and daily discloses himself in the whole workmanship of the universe. As a consequence, men cannot open their eyes without being compelled to see him."[4] Hence, we look to God, not from the outside, but we look to God from within.

As God's Spirit indwells our spirit, His Spirit transforms and renews our mind to be more and more like Christ Jesus; and with the mind of Christ, we therefore possess a natural knowledge of God that is revealed through faith. Here we have a relationship of faith and reason. We come to God, who is a God of *reason*, only through *faith*.

Beginning with the first commandment we find evidence for faith and reason. The verse states, *"And you shall love the Lord your God with all your heart, and with all your soul, and with all your mind, and with all your strength"* (Mark 12:30).

We can, therefore, say that faith is the divine work in us, and it changes us from sin and death to life in Christ. When we have God in our minds, His Spirit controls our attitudes and our behaviors; and when the Spirit of Christ is in control, we don't walk around seeking to be like everyone else around us; we are not to be conformed to the world. As Christian believers, we are now seeking to be who we really are as the Holy Spirit is transforming and renewing our minds, so we may prove what is that good and acceptable and perfect will of God.

While it is true we are saved through faith, there are two presuppositions for us to accept Him: We have to believe there is a God, and we have to believe that God rewards those who sincerely seek Him. According to Saint Augustine, "Faith is to believe what you do not see; the reward of this faith is to see what you believe."[5] Thus, you have to know about God in order to accept Him by faith. It is also critical that we understand that faith does not negate reason; it overrides reason.

Furthermore, A.M. Hunter wrote, "For St. Paul the Christian era is 'the dispensation of the Spirit,' the signs of which are 'freedom,' 'power' and 'joy.'"[6] So he sets the Christian life—its beginning, its middle, and its end—in the context of "the Spirit." Remember, our relationship with God is not physical, not material, not even intellectual; our relationship with God is spiritual.

You are to personally understand that God wants to communicate with you because He values your mind. Moreover, you are created in the image of God. This includes, among other attributes, the ability to reason; hence God also tells you, *"'Come now, and let us reason together,' says the Lord, 'Though your sins are as scarlet, they shall be white as snow; though they are red like crimson, they will be like wool'"* (Isa. 1:18). It is clear that the conflict is not between faith and reason, but between faith and sight.

ENDNOTES

1. Myles Munroe, *Rediscovering The Kingdom* (Shippensburg, PA: Destiny Image, Publishers, Inc., 2004), 30.

2. Aristotle, translated by David W. Graham, *Physics Book III* (Clarendon Press, 1999).

3. Peter Hanns Refil and Ellen Judy Wilson, *Encyclopedia of the Enlightenment* (New York, NY: Book Builders Inc. 1996), 443.

4. John Calvin, translated by Henry Beveridge, *Institutes of the Christian Religion*, accessed 25 August 2005; available from: www.ccel.org/c/calvin/chr_life/formats/christian_life1.0.doc.

5. St. Augustine, *Inspirational Quotes on Faith*, Internet: accessed 2 August 2005; available from: http://victoriastation.us/Hope%20Faith%202.htm.

6. A.M. Hunter, *Interpreting Paul's Gospel* (London, England: SCM Press LTD, 1954).

CHAPTER EIGHT

The Masquerade Is Over!

In order to understand both the negative and positive roles of the body in the spiritual life, and in life generally, we must take a deeper view of the nature of human personality, character, and action. It is quite evident that our environment teaches us to act like others around us. "Monkey see, monkey do," goes the proverb. It has also been proven that our environment influences personality development by as much as 50 percent, and it is largely for the good. But it also embeds in us habits of evil that permeate all human lives. This then influences the standard human patterns of responding to *"The lust of the flesh, and the lust of the eyes, and the boastful pride of life,"* which the apostle John said, *"is not from the Father but is from the world"* (1 John 2:16).

When you allow your mind to be conformed to the world, you then forsake the standard that God has established. Scripture tells us that God cautions in Jeremiah 2:13, *"For My people have committed two evils: They have forsaken Me, the fountain of living waters, to hew for themselves cisterns—broken cisterns that can hold no water."* Thus, sinful practices become the avenue for conforming to unacceptable standards and committing evil against God. Sinful practices become habits, then choices, and finally the character or the core of who you really are.

Other people may try to control you so you will conform to their desires. They might try to manipulate you in order to control you, until you become totally helpless under the bombardment of their thoughts, their concepts, and their desires. When this happens, you become lost in what other people expect of you until you no longer expect anything of yourself. You begin to act more like the person who is in control of your mind; you begin to take on the world's mannerism, the world's speech, the world's attitude until those things co-occupy your mind with so much of what they are, you don't even know that you have lost your original self—the real you.

CONFORMING TO CONTROLLING FORCES

As an original, living with a renewed mind, you are no longer a clone of anyone else. Do you remember the last conversation you had when you were in the middle of a battle and you said something that was completely out of character for you? You may have even used expressions and acted in ways that are not characteristic of you. Then you heard yourself say, "I am sorry; that was not really me." Who was it? You were expressing something that did not come from within; it came from your association, but it did not come from you. You did something that did not come from your mind. In essence, you were not expressing the power of who you are.

Likewise, you may have been involved in a relationship where you acted in ways that you didn't even know yourself. You may have asked yourself, "Why did this happen to me?" The answer is, you became totally helpless because of the bombardment of other people's thoughts, concepts, and desires, and you became lost in what other people expected of you until you no longer expected anything of yourself.

Subsequently, you realized that you took on an outward expression that did not come from the inside of you. And this is the crux of the word *conform*—it is not representative of the inner heart life. The prefix *con*, meaning "with" or "together," added to the Latin verb *formare*, meaning "to form," conveys the idea of assuming an expression that is patterned after something else.

Meanwhile, you may ask yourself another question: "How can I have any peace when I have allowed someone else to disconnect me from my mind, and then try to connect me to his or her controlling forces?" It must be crystal clear that when you disconnect yourself from your mind, and begin to focus on doing what the other person wants, you are then conforming your life and copying someone else.

This becomes complicated, because when you are not connected to the Spirit of Christ, you will assume the world's disposition, conforming to what others dictate. Consequently, when you give up your mind to the dictates of someone else, you become something that is not you. When you allow this to happen, the other person, while living and controlling his or her own destiny, is at the same time also controlling your mind and your destiny.

For example, two people are in an intimate relationship, such as marriage, and the relationship lasts for a long period of time. The partners become so attached to each other until they are of one mind. Then one person says, "I no longer need you," and the relationship ends. The query becomes, "Where do you go to get your original mind if you don't even know who you are?" You must be aware that when you give someone else control of your mind, you no longer have control of your life and destiny.

So, if you are not in control of your own mind, you are being controlled—according to the definition of *conformed*—by something or someone else. That means you are living a masquerade; you have picked up and copied the world's mannerisms, speech, expressions, and style. In essence, the other person's habits, attitude, and disposition have become imbedded in your mind. You have been conformed to the world's behaviors and standards.

RENEWED, REFRESHED, AND IN CONTROL

It is no secret, satan wants to control your innermost being and co-occupy your mind without you realizing that he is stealing the real, innermost being out of you. He seeks to make you more like him and his demons of the world. Yes, satan wants to control and manipulate every child of God. You must therefore be connected to the Living Water—the Spirit of Christ—who renews, refreshes, and transforms your mind so others cannot control you.

When you are transformed by the renewing of the mind, you can feel a wind blowing in your spirit as the Holy Spirit moves through your mind. And even though satan may attempt to control you, you will stand up and defy your environment because the Spirit of Christ is moving in you. And because you are connected to God's Spirit, you will resist conformity to the world and embrace the transformation that comes from Jesus Christ. Nevertheless, you must keep in mind that this transformation process does not happen overnight. So you will not express outwardly as quickly as what takes place on the inside. When God places something in your mind, it takes time for the environment to adjust to who you are. Again, if you are "in Christ," you are a new creature; old things have passed away (see 2 Cor. 5:17). You are in Christ, you have a new life, new attitude, new dreams, new power, new visions; and you are now walking in the power of God.

Moreover, it is with confidence that you can boldly say to the devil, "I don't need you. There was a time when I was under your control, and my broken spirit could not hold the water. When I tried to do what you wanted me to do, I got nowhere. When I tried to take on your mannerisms and sound like you, my mind was still stuck in sinful flesh. But now that I am in Christ, I am connected to the Living Water. I will not forsake the fountain of Living Water, and will not hewn myself cisterns—broken cisterns that can hold no water."

Just think about David fighting Goliath, and the mistake he would have made if he had put on Saul's armor. David knew that he could not wear Saul's armor into battle because it did not fit him. The only weapon he had was a slingshot—but an anointed slingshot. He needed nothing else. David was aware that he was connected to the Spirit of God, and that God ordered his steps. He did not need Saul's armor, nor did he need Goliath's sword. David knew that he did not have to adapt the mannerisms of his enemies. God had a plan, and David walked in His will. It was David who said, *"Eventhough I walk through the valley of the shadow of death, I fear no evil"* (see Ps. 23). He did not have to worry, for he was anointed with oil—the Holy Spirit. The Living Water was refreshing, renewing, and controlling his mind.

The Spirit of Christ, which indwells each believer, will cause you to bless others if you will be a living sacrifice of service. In Romans 12:1, Paul begs for the mercies of God because he saw the Light, the creative force; and he recognized that the Light in Christ is now embedded in the souls of men. In other words, he is really saying, "I beg you, I beg you please, I beg you by the mercies of God." With a new and transformed mind, you are as alive as a river of water, and you are not stale and stagnated like a pond. You can feel the Spirit of Christ—an original branch that is attached to the Vine; then you know that you are transformed with a renewed mind.

To comprehend the power of the mind that has been transformed and renewed, it is critical to understand the word "transfigured." The Greek verb, *metamorphoo,* is translated "transfigure" in the transfiguration narrative of Matthew 17:2 and Mark 9:2. The Scripture says that Jesus, the man of sorrow just like everybody else, walked up the mountain, and all of a sudden, He released in His mind the deity that He was. The Bible says, *"His face shone like the sun"* (see Matt.17:1-2). It was not a reflection of anything else; it was who He was on the inside. The only other place where the word "transfigured" appears in the New Testament is Second Corinthians 3:18, which mentions believers being "changed" into the likeness of Christ from one degree of glory to another by the operation of the Lord, who is the Spirit.

Remember, God created us for Himself, and He wants to bring out the beauties that He instilled in each of us. God wants you to know that He created each one of us as an original, and we belong to Him first. You must, therefore, open the valves of faith, and keep hope alive in your transformed and renewed mind. Just as light overtakes darkness, you can overtake this world system when you are "in Christ." God now wants His Living Water to flow within your mind so that goodness will flow from you like water from a pellucid spring. You must stir your faith, and stay connected to God's Spirit, through God's Word.

CHAPTER NINE

The Power of a Renewed Mind

God does not work through conformity. He is looking for evidence of real transformation—transformation that takes place only through the renewing of the mind. When the mind is renewed, you have the *"Have this attitude in yourselves which was also in Christ Jesus"* (see Phil. 2:5-8). With God's Spirit constantly flowing into your spirit, you will find that you are becoming more and more like Jesus; and by having the mind of Christ, you will also have some *"I AMness."* Scripture records Jesus boldly saying, "I AM the Truth; I AM the Light; I AM the Vine. I AM, I AM, I AM." The *"I AMness"* separates Him from everyone else. He was unique in His birth, life, and resurrection. He did not conform His life to the customs and traditions of the culture during His life on earth. For example it was against the custom and traditions when He spoke with the woman at the well and healed the sick on the Sabbath.

Likewise, when you have the mind of Christ, you will step into your *"I Amness"* and do what is not necessarily politically correct or traditional. We must walk in the Spirit, not in the flesh. Be in the world, not of the world. Then you can boldly say in your *"I AMness"*:

◆ I am released from satan and his demons.

◆ I am going to be what God created me to be.

- ◆ I am growing by the power of God, and the real me is about to be released.

- ◆ I am totally original; I am not a copy, and I cannot be duplicated.

- ◆ I am winning this mind game because God put winning in my spirit.

- ◆ I am going to overcome.

- ◆ I am an original blessing from God.

- ◆ I am going to stand up and claim what is mine.

Moreover, the mind is set on a higher level because we are renewed through our connection with the Holy Spirit. Then each of us can say, "Get the shackles off me. I am breaking out of these chains because I have been transformed by the renewing of my mind." Thus, satan no longer has control over you because the chains have been broken. You have stepped into the world, but you are not conformed to the world. You are transformed by the renewing of your mind, and with the Spirit of Christ connected to your spirit, you are a new creature—an original, which cannot be imitated or duplicated. *You* are in control of *your mind*.

You have victory in your mind, power in your mind, joy in my mind, and you are climbing to higher heights. You can walk in the world but not be governed by the environment and standards of the world. You have been created by God and the world can scrape through all the façade and look at the beautiful, powerful, joyful you—God's original and new creation.

YOU HAVE THE VICTORY

You are now walking in power because you have been transformed. The Spirit of the Lord is blowing into your spirit, and you are able to stand and defy your environment. It does not matter that you were once the greatest slave to satan and his demons. Satan can no longer control you because the fountain of Living Water is so far down in you that the devil cannot reach it.

With the Spirit of God connected to your mind, you have victory, and you shall overcome and have peace. You will have peace because the Bible says, *"The steadfast of mind You will keep in perfect peace, because he trusts in You"* (Isa. 26:3). God came and gave His life so that we might have life and have it more abundantly (see John 10:10).

Just remember, when you were bound by the world's attitudes and mannerisms, Jesus died and shed His blood to release you from sin and death. He went to hell and took the keys, then He stuck them in your hands and said, "Now, you open your own doors, you fix what's broken, and you straighten it out. I gave you the keys because I have made you like Me." You are now an emancipator and are slated for victory. You can boldly say, "I am expected to win the mind games; I am running with all my heart, and I am going to overcome and win because God put winning in my mind."

CHAPTER TEN

Theological and Philosophical Thoughts and Concepts

WE PERCEIVE GOD BY FAITH—THE HEART, NOT BY REASON	
THEOLOGY	PHILOSOPHY
The Bible gives us clarity to support the concept in both the Old and New Testaments. Scripture reveals that God is a God of reason, and He wants to communicate with us; however, God is Spirit, and we can come to God only in spirit and truth. REASON Isaiah 1:18—"'Come now, and let us reason together,' says the Lord, 'Though your sins are as scarlet, they will be white as snow; though they are red like crimson, they will be like wool.'" Daniel 2:20— "Let the name of God be blessed forever and ever, for wisdom and power belong to Him" First Corinthians 1:21—"For since in the wisdom of God the world through its wisdom did not come to know God, God was well-pleased through the foolishness of the message preached to save those who believe"	The origin of the argument "reasons for faith" is witnessed by an early challenge from Epicurus, a Greek philosopher of the 3rd century B.C. Epicurus claimed that all order and design in the universes arose from accidental joining of atoms; the Designer of the universe was "blind chance." Cicero retorted: "If anyone supposes that this most beautiful and glorious world was made by the accidental coming together of atoms, I do not understand why he should not suppose that the Annals of Ennius might be produced by pouring out on the earth the twenty-one letters of the alphabets in countless profusion."[1]

FAITH

Hebrews 11:6—*"And without faith it is impossible to please Him, for he who comes to God must believe that He is, and that He is a rewarder of those who seek Him."*

Ephesians 2:8—*"For by grace you have been saved through faith, and that not of yourselves; it is the gift of God."*

First Peter 3:15—*"But sanctify Christ as Lord in your hearts, always being ready to make a defense to everyone who asks you to give an account for the hope that is in you, yet with gentleness and reverence."*

A more philosophical argument for the existence of God is the Cosmological Argument, which is based on causality; the cause and effect relationship, to demonstrate the need for a subsistent (self-existent, uncreated) Being as the Initial Cause of all other things."[2]

Blaise Pascal — "It is the heart which perceives God and not the reason. That is what faith is: God perceived by the heart, not by the reason."[3]

Martin Luther — "All who call on God in true faith, earnestly from the heart, will certainly be heard, and will receive what they have asked and desired."[4]

Pascal —Thus wishing to appear openly to those who seek Him with all their heart and hidden from those who shun Him with all their heart, He has qualified our knowledge of Him by giving signs which can be seen by those who seek Him and not by those who do not. "Belief is a wise wager. Granted that faith cannot be proved, what harm will come to you if you gamble on its truth and it proves false? If you gain, you gain all; if you lose, you lose nothing. Wager, then, without hesitation, that He exists."[5]

Albert Einstein — "That deep emotional conviction of the presence of a superior reasoning power, which is revealed in the incomprehensible universe, forms my idea of God."[6]

Einstein — "I want to know all God's thoughts; all the rest are just details."[7]

	Einstein — "My religion consists of a humble admiration of the illimitable superior spirit who reveals himself in the slight details we are able to perceive with our frail and feeble mind."[8]
	Saint Augustine — "Faith is to believe what you do not see; the reward of this faith is to see what you believe."[9]
	Saint Augustine — "Seek not to understand that you may believe, but believe that you may understand."[10]
	Saint Augustine — "Faith is a living, daring confidence in God's grace, so sure and certain that a man could stake his life on it a thousand times."[11]
	Paul Tillich — "Faith consists in being vitally concerned with that ultimate reality to which I give the symbolical name of God. Whoever reflects earnestly on the meaning of life is on the verge of an act of faith."[12]

ENDNOTES

1. Cited in *Reasons for Faith*, "A Catholic Response, Inc.," accessed 12 September 2005; available from: http:users.binary.net/polycarp/reasons.html.

2. Cited in *Reasons for Faith*, "A Catholic Response, Inc.," accessed 12 September 2005; available from: http:users.binary.net/polycarp/reasons.html.

3. Blaise Pascal, *Pensees* (London, England: Penguin Group), 127.

4. Martin Luther, translated by R. Bente and W.H.T. Dan "The Large Catechism," cited in the Project Wittenberg, accessed 18 June 2005; available from:

http://www.iclnet.org/pub/resources/text/wittenberg/
luther/catechism/web/cat-04.html.

5. Blaise Pascal, *Pensees* (London, England: Penguin Group).
121.

6. Albert Einstein, *The New Quotable Einstein*, ed. Alice
Calaprice, (Princeton, NJ: Princeton University Press,
2005). 198.

7. Ibid., 194.

8. Ibid., 195.

9. Saint Augustine "The Four Virtues," accessed 25 June
2005; available from: http://www.thefourvirtues.com/
fourvirtues/peop;e/Saint_Augustine/Saint/_Augustine.a
sp.

10. Ibid.

11. Ibid.

12. Paul Tillich, *A History of Christian Thought*, ed. Carle E.
Braaten (New York: Simon and Schuster, 1968), 387.

Meanings and Explanations With Use and Application

BESEECH (GK: *PARAKALEO*\PAR-AK-AL-EH)

STRONG #3870: to call near, i.e. invite, invoke (by imploration, hortation or consolation): beseech, call for, (be of good) comfort, desire, (give) exort (-ation), intreat, pray.

VINE: Denotes "to call to one's side," hence, "to call to one's aid."

WEBSTER: To beg for urgently or anxiously; to request earnestly; to implore; to make supplication.

USE AND APPLICATION: Beseech is to call to one's aid. It is used for every kind of calling to a person which is meant to produce a particular effect, hence, with various meanings, such as "comfort, exhort, desire, call for," in addition to its significance "to beseech," which has a stronger force than to ask. The law says, "I command you," but grace says, "I beseech you."

CONFORMED (GK: *SUSCHEMATIZÇ*\SOOS-KHAY-MAT-ID-ZO)

STRONG # 4964: To fashion alike, i.e. conform to the same pattern; conform to, fashion self according to. Denoting union; with or together; i.e. by association, companionship, process, resemblance, possession.

VINE: "To fashion or shape one thing like another,"...This verb has more especial reference to that which is transitory, changeable, unstable; to that which is essential in character and thus complete or durable, not merely a form or outline.

WEBSTER: To give the same shape, outline, or contour to: bring into harmony or accord; to be similar or identical or to act in accordance with prevailing standards or customs.

USE AND APPLICATION: To conform one's self (i.e. one's mind and character) to another's pattern, (fashion one's self according to) "Be not Conformed" Paul is saying, "Don't let the world squeeze you into its mold!" Don't be molded by the mannerisms, speech, expressions, styles and habits of this world! Kenneth Wuest has paraphrased the verse as follows: "Stop assuming an outward expression which is patterned after this world, an expression which does not come from, nor is it representative of what you are in your inner being as a regenerated child of God."[1]

HOLY (GK: *HAGIOS*\HAG-EE-OSS)

STRONG #40: The state of purity, and is always refer sanctification, Sacred, pure, blameless, consecrated: (most) holy (one, thing), saint.

VINE: Fundamentally signifies "separated" (among the Greeks, dedicated to the gods), and hence, in Scripture in its moral and spiritual significance, separated form sin and therefore consecrated to God, sacred. It is predicated of God (as the absolutely "Holy" One, in His purity, majesty and glory).

WEBSTER: Exalted or worthy of complete devotion as one perfect in goodness and righteousness; Divine for the Lord our God is holy; devoted entirely to deity or the work of deity; and having a divine quality.

USE AND APPLICATION: A holy God calls for a holy people. Holiness is separation from everything profane and defiling; and at the same time, it is dedication to everything holy and pure. People or even objects, such as anointing oil or vessels, may be considered holy to the Lord—set apart for God's holy will and service. God's people are "saints," set apart for the service of the King of Kings! Do you see yourself as a holy servant of the Most High God?

MERCY / MERCIES (GK: *OIKTIRMOS*\OYK-TIR-MOS)

STRONG #3628: To have pity on; compassion, mercy; bowels in which compassion resides, a heart of compassion; emotions, longings, manifestations of pity. The point established is that the "mercy" and compassion shown by God are determined by nothing external to His attributes. By the "mercies of God"—this is not the same word for mercy which is found in Rom.11:30-32, but the idea is similar. It means "pity, mercy, compassion."

VINE: "Pity, compassion for the ills of others," is used (a) of God, Who is *"the Father of mercies,"* 2 Cor. 1:3; His "mercies" are the ground upon which believers are to present their bodies a living sacrifice, holy acceptable to God, as their reasonable service, Romans 12:1.

WEBSTER: price paid, wages; compassion that forbears punishment even when justice demands it; a blessing that is an act of divine favor or compassion; grace of God.

USE AND APPLICATION: God has been so compassionate and merciful to us and He wants us to show mercy and compassion toward all who are weak and defenseless. God sets the example by His constant compassion for the helpless and undeserving (see Isaiah 54:8,10).

MIND (GK: *NOUS*\NOOCE)

STRONG #3563: Verb to "know" it denotes the faculty of knowing, the seat of understanding, reasoning, and thinking ability. From the base of ginosko (#1097) form of the primary verb; to "know."

VINE: Denotes speaking generally, the seat of reflective consciousness, comprising the faculties of perception and understanding, and those of feeling, judging and determining. Its use in the New Testament may be analyzed the faculty of knowing, the seat of understanding, counsels, purpose, (of the mind of God; of the thoughts and counsels of God).

WEBSTER: the element or complex of elements in an individual that feels, perceives, thinks, wills, and esp. reasons.

USE AND APPLICATION: Your mind can only be renewed through the creative work of the Holy Spirit when your spirit is connected to the Spirit through the Word or study of the Scriptures.

PRESENT YOUR BODIES (GK: PARISTEM\PAR-IS-TAY-MEE)

STRONG #3936: from beside to stand, i.e. (trans.) to exhibit, offer, (spec.) recommend, (fig.) substantiate; or (intrans.) to be at hand (or ready) aid: assist, bring before, command, commend, give presently, present, prove, provide, sew, stand before, by, here, up, with), yield.

VINE: Denotes, when used transitively, "to place beside" (para, "by," histemi, "to set"), "to present," e.g. Romans 6:13 "yield."

WEBSTER: to bring or introduce into the presence of someone esp. of superior rank or status; to give or bestow formally; to lay (as a charge) before a court as an object of inquiry; and to offer to view.

USE AND APPLICATION: "Present your bodies." When you give God your body you are giving Him all that you are and all that you have. The verb "present" is in the aorist tense, which simply means *"Do it!"*

RENEW, RENEWING
(GK: *ANAKAINÇSIS*\AN-AK-AH EE-NO-SIS)

STRONG #342: "renovation: renewing; new; freshness; regenerate.

VINE: akin "to make new" a renewal is used in Romans 12:2, "the renewing (of your mind)," i.e., the adjustment of the moral and spiritual vision and thinking to the mind of God, which is designed to have a transforming effect on the life.

WEBSTER: To make new spiritually: regenerate: to restore to existence; to make extensive changes in; and to begin again.

USE AND APPLICATION: The renewing of the mind is the adjustment of the moral and spiritual vision and thinking to the mind of God, which is designed to have a transforming effect upon the life. This passage stresses the willing response on the part of the believer.

SACRIFICE (GK: *THUSIA*\THOO-SEE-AH)

STRONG #2378: From (#2380) to rush (breathe hard, blow, smoke), i.e. (by impl.) to sacrifice; to immolate (slaughter for any purpose); kill, do sacrifice, slay; from sacrifice (the act or the victim, literally or figuratively).

VINE: Primarily denotes "the act of offering"; then, objectively, "that which is offered" of animal or other "sacrifices," as offered under the Law; of Christ, in His "sacrifice" on the cross; of the body of the believer, presented to God as a living "sacrifice."

WEBSTER: An act of offering to a deity something precious.

USE AND APPLICATION: When we think of sacrifice, it usually suggests merely an inconvenience or the giving of a costly gift. In Hebrew it involves the offering of a life.

TRANSFORMED
(GK: *METAMORPHOÇ*\MET-AM-OR-FRO) TRANSFORM

STRONG #3339: (lit. or fig.) "metamorphose" change, transfigure, transform; to fashion (through the idea of adjustment of parts); shape; fig. Nature – form.

VINE: (lit. transfigure) "to change into another form" (meta, implying change, and morph, "form." Is used in the passive voice (a) of Christ's transfiguration.

WEBSTER: To change in composition or structure; to change the outward form or appearance; to change in character or condition: convert; to become transformed: change—transformable.

USE AND APPLICATION: Transformed: This is the ancient Greek word *metamorphoo*—describing a metamorphosis. The same word is used to describe Jesus in His transfiguration (see Mark 9:2-3). This is a glorious transformation! To be transformed, however, denotes renewal; "the renewing (of your mind);" the adjustment of the moral and spiritual vision and thinking to the mind of God, which is designed to have a transforming effect upon the life. The transformation process that takes place in the believer's mind causes you to become more and more conformed to the image of Christ.

WORLD (GK: -*AION*\AHEE-OHN)

STRONG #165: "An age, a period of time," marked in the New Testament usage by spiritual or moral characteristics, is sometimes translated "world"; the RV marg. always has "age." In Second Corinthians 4:4 we learn that satan is the "god of this world (age)." Christ gave Himself for our sins, that He might deliver us from this present evil world (age) Galatians 1:4. When we were unsaved we were a part of this evil, satanic age/world, but God has delivered us out of it.

VINE: "An age, a period of time," marked in the New Testament usage by spiritual or spiritual characteristics, is sometimes translated "world." In Romans 12:2, "world" is relating to its fashion.

WEBSTER: Human existence, a earthly state of human existence; life after death—used with a qualifier [the next] the earth with its inhabitants and all things upon it; individual course of life.

USE AND APPLICATION: As a believer, you are taught by grace to live godly in this present age. We are *in* this world, but we are not to live as those who are *of* this world and who are part of this world system, which is in opposition to the true and living God.

ENDNOTE

1. Wuest, Kenneth S. *Wuest's Word Studies in the Greek New Testament*. CD-ROM. Grand Rapids: Eerdmans, 1997.

Practical Applications

It is clear that with a transformed and renewed mind you are laying aside your own desires to be of service. *"And do not neglect doing good and sharing, for with such sacrifices God is pleased"* (Heb. 13:16). It is important that you think of some specific applications and reflections to apply both the theological and philosophical lessons learned to correctly understand:

- ◆ Our connection to God is based on faith, not reason.

- ◆ The conflict is not between faith and reason, but between faith and sight.

- ◆ Transformation takes place in the mind.

ACTION STEPS

Actions to take or things you can do in order let God's Word and His Holy Spirit maintain control of your transformed and renewed mind:

A. Prayerfully and carefully read Romans 12:1-2; Hebrews 10:19–13:25.

B. Show that you have faith by believing in God's promises, because God will do what He says He will do:

1. Celebrate daily that you have gained access to God through the shed blood of Jesus Christ. Tell others what God has done or is doing in your life and give thanks to God for everything—even the small things.

2. Have complete confidence and belief in God. Let the Word shape your thinking. Apply God's Word directly to your situations—insert your name in the text as you read the Scripture and let the Word speak directly to you and your specification situations and issues.

3. Do not worry. Pray and trust God; He will fulfill His promises, even when you don't see any evidence.

4. Seek God diligently through prayer and meditation, and believe that He will reward you for it.

5. Practice persistent and patient praise.

6. Sing a hymn or song that reminds you to trust and praise Him for guiding you: *"Through Him then, let us continually offer up a sacrifice of praise to God, that is, the fruit of lips that give thanks to His name"* (Heb. 13:15).

7. Read First Peter 2:5 to understand that by the renewing of your mind, your body is now a temple—a spiritual house, a thank-offering to God.

8. Read Romans 13:21 to understand that with your new mind, your relationship to the world has changed.

9. Behave like a Christian in every part of your life—job, activities, recreation, attitudes, giving, shopping, dancing, eating, talking.

PERSONAL GROWTH AND DEVELOPMENT

- Spend daily time with God through the Word.
- Pray and meditate upon God's Word that your basic thinking patterns are being changed and that you gain the mind of Christ.

◆ Seek God's will so you know what He wants, and then do what is good and pleasing to God.

You are called to a different lifestyle than what the world offers with its behavior and customs. You are now living according to the essential nature of the spiritual mind; hence you are now required to:

◆ Love without hypocrisy.

◆ Abhor what is evil.

◆ Cling to what is good.

◆ Be kind and affectionate to one another.

◆ Serve the Lord.

◆ Rejoice in hope and be patient in tribulation.

◆ Pray continually.

◆ Give to the needs of others.

◆ Live peacefully with others.

◆ Love your enemy.

A. Read and memorize Mark 12:29-31 and First Peter 3:15. Remember, God gave you a mind and He expects you to use it.

B. Read and study the Word so that you can glorify God by sharing the Gospel with others.

C. Memorize verses from the Scriptures so you are always ready to give a testimony and defense to everyone who asks for the reason you have hope (faith) in God.

D. Believe that Jesus is Lord, so you can say, as C.S. Lewis said, "I believe in Christianity as I believe that the sun has risen; not only because I see it, but because by it I see everything else."[1]

E. Live your life and govern your actions by your belief; it is through faith that you have committed yourself to Christ and He is your personal Savior.

F. The following Scriptures are valuable tools for assurance that faith is your personal trust in God: Romans 1:17; 3:22; 14:22; 2 Corinthians 5:7; Galatians 3:5; Ephesians 2:8; 6:16; 2 Timothy 4:7; 1 Peter 3:15; 1 Corinthians 1:21; and Isaiah 1:18.

G. Other scriptural references for understanding and experiencing transformation from the inside out: Romans 8:28-29; 12:1-2; 1 John 1:5-6; John 13:35; 1 Corinthians 2; 2 Corinthians 10:3-4; Ephesians 4:22-24.

ENDNOTE

1. C.S. Lewis, "Is Theology Poetry?" *The Weight of Glory and other Addresses* (New York: Harper Collins Publishers, 1980), 140.

Section Two

Enjoying Freedom in Christ

Enjoying Freedom in Christ

Freedom is critical to experiencing the kind of life that God has always intended for you. In this section, you will discover that the freedom you seek will come through ways that are antithetical to most everything you thought.

Jesus came to set men and women free. *"And you will know the truth, and the truth will make you free"* (John 8:32). *"The Spirit of the Lord is upon Me, because He anointed Me to preach the gospel to the poor. He has sent Me to proclaim release to the captives, and recovery of sight to the blind, to set free those who are oppressed"* (Luke 4:18). His way to freedom is much different than what we presuppose. The postmodern world's attempt at freedom is to fight for our rights, insist on our ways, and demand that people respect our space. These things might give the semblance of freedom, but they do not provide real freedom.

Jesus came to reverse the natural order that exists in both the secular and the spiritual world. In His world, the last is first, the least is the greatest, and the humble finds grace. Humility is the pathway to this freedom, and worship is the expression of that freedom.

A New Model for the Mind—Truth From the Book of Philippians

We begin Parts Three and Four by noting that in Philippians chapters 2 and 4, Paul is very conscious to leave us with the lesson of the strength and power (dunamis; exousia) of the mind. Paul says to the Philippians, *"Have this attitude in yourselves which was also in Christ Jesus"*(Phil. 2:5).

The Book of Philippians is a book of rejoicing, of giving God accolades, and giving God praise. While writing this book of joy and rejoicing, Paul was incarcerated and was waiting to face Nero, that egomaniac and narcissist fellow. Eventually, because of the judgment of Nero, Paul was martyred for the cause of Christ Jesus.

Even at this very critical time in his life, Paul continues to write to a group of people who are free, and proclaims to them the joy that they ought to have because of their relationship with God. The apostle Paul also conveys his love and gratitude for the believers at Philippi as well as exhorts them to a lifestyle of unity, holiness, and joy. Philippians is filled with commendation, encouragement, gratitude, love, and joy. At the same time, this book provides practical application for thanksgiving, rejoicing, and praising the Lord in the midst of adverse circumstances.

Paul was also seeking to correct a problem with disunity and rivalry by urging all believers to imitate Christ in His humility and servanthood. He instructs that we are to be of the same mind, rejoice always, and pray about everything. When we follow the instructions given to the Church, we will experience true *joy*, by putting Jesus first, Others second, and You last. Hence, *JOY* = Jesus, Others, You.

As the apostle urges believers to have the same mind (attitude) as Christ, he reveals much about Jesus Christ as the Son of God as well as Jesus Christ as Lord. Jesus is presented as the model of true humility as He willingly laid aside His heavenly glory to come to earth and die.

We must understand that His incarnation, humiliation, and obedience not only led Him to the Cross, but also ultimately exalted Him to the highest place and gives Him a name that is above all names. God said, *"So that at the name of Jesus EVERY KNEE WILL BOW, of those who are in heaven and on earth and under the earth, and that every tongue will confess that Jesus Christ is Lord, to the glory of God the Father"* (Phil. 2:10-11).

From a historical perspective, the theme of the Book of Philippians is the "all sufficiency of Christ" (Gk: *autarkei*). The Greek concept is self-satisfaction, or always enough. Paul could therefore say, "I don't have to worry about anything; I can rejoice because God is always enough."

Paul was obviously so deeply rooted in God, that no matter what was happening in his life, he kept his mind on Christ Jesus. It is important to note that Paul's life was sharply divided into two parts by his conversion. Before his conversion, he was a furious persecutor of Christians, but his life was overturned when Christ appeared to him on his way to Damascus. He immediately lost his sight, and after three days of blindness, he was told that he would suffer many things for Christ's sake (see Acts 9:15-16). Besides the many persecutions, Paul also had to bear an infirmity or a thorn in the flesh (see I Cor. 12:7). In addition, he was bitten by a poisonous snake (see Acts 28:3). Paul summarized many of his other sufferings:

"Three times I was beaten with rods, once I was stoned, three times I was shipwrecked, a night and a day I have spent in the deep. I have been on frequent journeys, in dangers from rivers, dangers from robbers, dangers

from my countrymen, dangers from the Gentiles, dangers in the city, dangers in the wilderness, dangers on the sea, dangers among false brethren; I have been in labor and hardship, through many sleepless nights, in hunger and thirst, often without food, in cold and exposure. Apart from such external things, there is the daily pressure on me of concern for all the churches" (2 Corinthians 11:25-28).

His perseverance and strength is to be admired, for many of us would be inclined to become depressed during trials and tribulations, especially if we are serving God as vehemently and audaciously as Paul served Him throughout his life. But when we know God as Paul knew Him, we can lift Him up no matter what we are experiencing in our lives.

In chapter 1 of Philippians Paul explains to the believers that they shouldn't despair over his imprisonment because what has happened to him is helping spread the Gospel; and his experiences in prison are stimulating and encouraging other believers to willingly take a stand for Christ and preach the Gospel regardless of the consequences. He says, *"Now I want you to know, brethren, that my circumstances have turned out for the greater progress of the gospel, so that my imprisonment in the cause of Christ has become well known throughout the whole praetorian guard and to everyone else, and that most of the brethren, trusting in the Lord because of my imprisonment, have far more courage to speak the word of God without fear"* (Phil. 1:12-14). Essentially, he is telling us that when we have the mind of Christ, we can face anything simply because of the strength of our mind. Why? Paul knew that as long as his mind was connected to Christ, he would be able to overcome all trials and tribulations.

Every believer needs to see God from a position of *"I AM always enough."* We need to know that the Most High God is saying to each and every one of us:

◆ I AM enough when you have nothing.

◆ I AM enough to heal you.

◆ I AM enough to deliver you.

◆ I AM enough when everyone is against you.

- ◆ I AM enough when you don't have money.
- ◆ I AM enough for whatever you need.

Paul is actually saying, "My life is not my own; it belongs to Christ. If I die, I will be out of this body, and with the Lord." Without a doubt, we are to mirror Paul's attitude by saying, "What can you do worse to me than take my life? If I am not afraid to die, then surely I will rejoice and enjoy my life." Paul understood the value of knowing that God is sufficient. He said, *"We are of good courage, I say, and prefer rather to be absent from the body and to be at home with the Lord"* (2 Cor. 5:8).

The apostle Paul was not the kind of guy to hang out with if you didn't have the same commitment that he possessed. Just think how you would feel if you were locked in a cell with Paul in a Roman prison, and you want him to be quiet, but he wants to keep talking about Jesus. At the same time, you know that Nero is killing Christians and feeding them to the lions. To this day, you can still visit the great coliseum in Rome where Christians were burned and devoured by lions for entertainment at sports events. If you were cell mates with Paul when he was talking about Christ Jesus, you might want to say, "It's all right to pray quietly, Paul, but let's not have any big discussions about how living is Christ and dying is gain." But Paul had no problem saying just that—*"For me to live is Christ, and to die is gain"* (Phil. 1:21). Paul's attitude was, "I don't care what Caesar is doing; I don't care what the emperor is doing; I am going to enjoy my God."

Every child of God should be able to say, "If God brought me from the dead once, then the devil can't scare me with the threat of dying." If we came out of the trenches once, satan can't tell us when or how we should praise our God. It is far better to have the devil angry because we are praising God, then for us not to praise God in order to keep the devil happy. If the devil is chasing you, you can run into God's arm; but where do you go if God is coming after you? Our circumstances should never dictate the quality of our relationship with God; we are to praise God at all times. Psalm 34:1 says, *"I will bless the Lord at all times; His praise shall continually be in my mouth."* Our circumstances should never dictate the quality of our praise and relationship with God.

When we compare our situations or circumstances to the mountains and valleys that others are experiencing, we may discover that our biggest problem is very small. There are some people, no matter how low they sink in the valley of sickness, pain, suffering, persecutions, and tribulations, they are still able to experience more joy than others who may be living at the highest pinnacle of fame and fortune in their lives.

The conclusion is that no matter how far one man climbs on the highest mountain, or how low another man falls to the deepest valley of pain and suffering, neither circumstance will determine how much he will praise the Lord.

As Christian believers, we ought to be so high in our praises that even when we are at the lowest point in our lives, we can still find enough strength and faith to say, *"I will bless the Lord at all times; His praise shall continually be in my mouth"* (Ps. 34:1). As we encourage someone else and say, "In the name of Jesus, come on up a little higher," we can also say as Peter said, *"But Peter said, "I do not possess silver and gold, but what I do have I give to you: In the name of Jesus Christ the Nazarene--walk!""* (Acts 3:6).

PART THREE

A New Mind

The first key to freedom is acquiring a new mind. Paul told the Roman church that transformation was dependent upon obtaining a renewed mind. Your thinking determines your actions. Negative thinking will enslave you and steal your freedom.

Because the old mind has been corrupted by sin, negativity, and rejection, it doesn't need just a little change here and there; it needs a total overhaul. Getting a new mind is a process. Once you begin to experience this new way of thinking, you will begin to enjoy a new way of living.

CHAPTER ELEVEN

Achieving Unity Through Humility

PAUL'S MESSAGE—HAVING THE SAME MIND

In chapter 2 of Philippians, Paul presents a case for unity to the people of the church in Philippi. Paul declares that in order to gain unity, there must be humility. He deals with the concept of humility in verse 5 after he argumentatively suggests in verse 1 that there is consolation in Christ: *"Therefore if there is any encouragement in Christ, if there is any consolation of love, if there is any fellowship of the Spirit, if any affection and compassion"* (Phil. 2:1). While each "if" (Gk: *ei*) seems to be a subjunctive, it is not; *"ei,"* the word for "if" in the Greek concept, is actually declaring a condition that exists. Thus, each "if" in Philippians 2:1 should be translated to "because." Verse 1 would then read, "Because there is consolation in Christ, because there is comfort of love, because we have fellowship of the Spirit, because there are affections of mercy." Paul is actually saying, "As Christians, we have appeal in our union with Christ Jesus because *we have* consolation in Christ; *we have* comfort of love; *we have* fellowship of the Spirit; and *we have* affection of mercies.

Paul dearly loved and appreciated the Philippians, and he shared great joy with them. So he now brings the church from rejoicing to the idea of exaltation and unity. He begins with, *"Fulfill my joy"* (Gk: *chara*) by being *"greatly and exceedingly joyful."* He feels that he will have even more joy, and that his joy will be made full or complete if all the members are working together in unity and love by being likeminded. In looking at the word "likeminded" in both Hebrew and Greek, we find that this word (Heb: *isopsuchos*) literally means "of equal soul." It comes from two words—*isos*, meaning "equal," and *psuche*, meaning "the soul." The Greek concept of "likeminded" (Gk: *homophron*) is taken from the words *homo*, "the same," and *phren*, "the mind," or think the same thing. It means, "thinking the same thing" (present tense—continuously thinking of having the same love and unity of affection). Thus, we are to love the same things, love the Lord, and have the same love for one another. When he says, *"being of one accord* [Gk: *sumpsuchos*], *with united spirits,"* he is asking for unity of sentiment and for the members to think and act as if they are but one soul, one mind.

Scripture shows that the apostle Paul asked for unity at other churches as well. To the church at Corinth he writes, *"Now I exhort you, brethren, by the name of our Lord Jesus Christ, that you all agree and that there be no divisions among you, but that you be made complete in the same mind and in the same judgment"* (I Cor. 1:10). In the letter to the Romans he writes, *"Now may the God who gives perseverance and encouragement grant you to be of the same mind with one another according to Christ Jesus, so that with one accord you may with one voice glorify the God and Father of our Lord Jesus Christ"* (Rom. 15:5-6).

God is also appealing for unity in the Church today. It will bring great joy when the members are thinking the same thoughts—to love one another, to be likeminded, having the same love, and being of one accord. We are not to let petty quarrels and dissensions bring division among the members.

In essence, Paul's request is that we must be of one mind and equal soul as we seek to maintain unity with each other. It is through the love of Jesus Christ that our souls are united, our hearts are in unison, and we can truly live together in love as though we have one mind and one spirit between us.

Paul takes us to another level of thinking when he introduces the concept of humility in verse 3. He instructs that we are to humble ourselves, let go of our own pride, and turn away from selfish ambition or conceited attitudes in order to consider the needs of others. He admonishes that we are not to seek personal aggrandizement, but to esteem others as being more important and more worthy than oneself. We are family in the Lord, sharing the same Holy Spirit, and our hearts are to be tender and sympathetic at all times.

A HUMBLE MIND

Plato and other philosophers have enquired whether humility is a virtue; but virtue or not, they have agreed that nothing is more rare than lowliness of mind. The Greeks called it *tapeinosis* or *tapeineia*— "lowliness of mind."

- ◆ Plato strongly recommended in the fourth book of the Laws of Plato where he rejects the proud and would multiply the humble.[1]

- ◆ John Calvin maintains, "All the blessings we enjoy are Divine deposits, commited to our trust on this condition, that they should be dispensed for the benefit of our neighbors."[2]

- ◆ John Lock says, "To love our neighbor as ourselves is such a truth of regulating human society, that by that alone one might determine all the cases in social morality."[3]

It is from both theology and philosophy that we are admonished to work together as a Church to fulfill the commission that God has given us—to love one another and to "be of humble mind, laying aside all haughtiness, and pride, and foolishness, and angry feelings...being especially mindful of the words of the Lord Jesus which He spoke, teaching us meekness and long suffering."[4]

When we look at what's happening in churches today, we find that some people have been alienated from church because it has become a battleground of conflict that has nothing to do with the Gospel. Most conflicts among Christians are rooted in self-centeredness; fights and quarrels, caused, not by some external source, but by the people's evil desires. Disagreements often come about because members, deacons, elders, and sometimes even pastors, seek positions of power and status. Consequently, when everyone seeks his or her own pleasure, only strife and hatred result. Selfish ambition leads to division and strife, and thus creates different moods, different spirits, and different attitudes throughout the sanctuary.

In addressing conflicts among the members, the Bible says:

> *"What is the source of quarrels and conflicts among you? Is not the source your pleasures that wage war in your members?-- Or do you think that the Scripture speaks to no purpose: 'He jealously desires the Spirit which He has made to dwell in us'? But He gives a greater grace Therefore it says, 'GOD IS OPPOSED TO THE PROUD, BUT GIVES GRACE TO THE HUMBLE'"* (James 4:1,5-6).

James calls for believers to humble themselves. True faith is humility. And humility is the opposite of the proud selfishness and self-centered ambition that characterizes this present evil age. When disagreements occur in the church, we are to be wise enough to understand how to handle them correctly with godly wisdom.

The Word is clear—pride promotes strife, but humility can cure worldliness. Humility must be expressed in order to gain unity. And in order to have unity, you must be willing to offer yourself to meet the needs of others. For example, if participants in the music ministry want to sing melodiously and uniformly, they must attend rehearsals. The members must give up something and make adjustments to their lives and schedules in order to dedicate themselves to the rehearsals. If, however, the music ministers adopt the attitude, "I will go to rehearsal only when it is convenient for me," they will never have a unified voice. Why? When people act as individuals in a collective environment, it creates problems, defeating teamwork and effective group participation. The individual members will have to humble themselves for the benefit of the group.

We must cultivate a spirit of Christian humility and regard one another as more important than ourselves. Paul admonishes that we must not only be concerned about our interests, but we must be concerned about the interests of others. He tells us that we need to do the right thing even when we think no one is looking. He says, *"So then, my beloved, just as you have always obeyed, not as in my presence only, but now much more in my absence, work out your own salvation with fear and trembling"* (Phil. 2:12). We must love the people who come into the church because it is the right thing to do; we must humble ourselves, and treat each other with love and dignity because the consolation we have in Christ is an incentive and motivation for unity in the Holy Spirit.

OUR COMMON BOND IS JESUS

Paul advises that the Holy Spirit, the power of God, will move more vigorously in the Church if there is fellowship of the Spirit. When there is fellowship of the Spirit, there is joint participation among all the members in things that are common to each other. Fellowship of the Spirit causes the members to be likeminded, have the same love, be of one accord, of one mind so that there can be joint participation in things that are common to each other. When he says, "this joint participation in things that are common to each other," he is giving us the definition of "fellowship" (Gk: *koinonia*), which is, sharing in unity or shared by all. In order for there to be fellowship and joint participation, there must be agreement on a common or central purpose, and the one thing that is common among believers in the church is *Jesus*.

When we come together and call on the name of Jesus, it does not matter if one person eloquently describes Him and another person says His name in a simple dialect; as long as we are together as one and keep our minds on the Lord Jesus, the devil can't break up the house of God. Likewise, when the storms of life begin to rage in our homes and personal situations, we are to assemble our mates, children, and family members together to touch and agree in the name of Jesus. The devil cannot move against the house and family who focuses on the Lord because *"For where two or three have gathered together in My name, I am there in their midst"* (Matt. 18:20).

Because it is God's desire for love and harmony to permeate the church congregation, we must live unselfishly, and turn away from selfish ambitions or conceited attitudes. We must maintain unity with other believers in our thoughts, attitudes, love, spirit, and purpose. And where there is unity, the members of the church will have one thing in common—the Lord Jesus as Savior and the devil as the enemy.

Paul says there are some among the believers who are not controlled by the Holy Spirit. Hence, when the Lord moves through the Church, we don't recognize Him because we are not focused on Him. But God says, "If I can get two or three to touch and agree (focus on Me), I will be in their midst." The Holy Spirit will let the devil know that he cannot claim this territory because the members' minds are stayed on Christ Jesus. Jesus is the star in the household of faith, and when Jesus is the star, the Holy Spirit will destroy everything the devil is attempting to do.

The question now becomes: If each saint is indwelled by the Holy Spirit, why is there not unity among the saints? The answer is clear: It's not by virtue of the indwelling of the Holy Spirit; it's by virtue of His control of your life. Yes, you can be indwelled by the Holy Spirit a long time before the Spirit has control of you; and there is a difference. In many circumstances people can struggle to achieve a higher height in God, yet the Spirit of God has no control in their lives. And so, the Church can be easily infiltrated with rifts and divisions, and where there are rifts and divisions, the doors are opened for warring, fighting, and contentious attitudes.

If only the Church would come together and touch and agree to focus on Jesus. When the Spirit of Christ is in control of our lives, we are able to work out the struggles and disagreements because the Holy Spirit directs us, guides, and leads us through what is significant in our lives. The Holy Spirit has a way of removing insignificant matters from our minds and wills; then He causes us to fellowship with people who have a common purpose. In other words, when we come to kneel together, to pray together, to praise together, and to worship together, we have one thing in common—Christ Jesus is our Savior who provides an example of a sacrificial and humble mind, and the devil is our enemy.

ENDNOTES

1. Plato, translator Benjamin Jowett "Laws" cited from *Book IV*, The Classis Library HTML edition, 2000. accessed 12 September 2005.

2. John Calvin, translated by Henry Bevridge "On the Christian Life" Institute of the Christian Religion, accessed 18 June 2005; available from: www.ccel.org/c/**calvin**/chr_life/formats/christian_life1. 0.doc.

3. John Locke, *An Essay Concerning the True Origin, Extent and End of Civil Government* (1990), accessed 8 February 2005 available from: http://www.cleverlely.org/areopagus/docs/locke/locke3htm.

4. Clement of Rome "An Exhortation to Humility" From the First Epistle of Clement to the Corinthians, prepared by Pontifical Theological Faculty "Marianum Rome, 2001, accessed 18 June 2005; available from: http://www.vatican.va/spirit/documents/spirit_20010627_clement_en.html. Note: Excerpts are public domain.

CHAPTER TWELVE

Exchanging Your Mind for God's Mind

Paul presents Jesus as a perfect example of unselfishness and instructs, *"Let this mind be in you which was also in Christ Jesus."* Jesus Christ is our example of the sacrificial mind, the serving mind, the humble mind, and the mind of love. When you have the mind of Christ, you have the indwelling of the Holy Spirit, the indwelling of the Father and the Son in your transformed and renewed mind. And with the mind of Christ, you should be willing to adopt Christ's attitude of love, unselfishness, servanthood, humility, and obedience, looking beyond our own interest for the sake of others.

Humility is not a problem when you love. Most of us humble ourselves from time to time—usually to the ones we love. For example, two ladies lived next door to each other for many years. One lady rose at three o'clock in the morning and looked through the window and saw that her neighbor was in the kitchen. Later that day she asked, "What were you doing up at three o'clock this morning?" The neighbor responded, "I was cooking for my husband; he had just gotten home." "You got up at three to cook for your husband?" the nosey neighbor asked and continued, "I would never get up at three o'clock to cook for anybody." The wife then responded, "I love my husband and I will get up at anytime to cook for him."

When love is in place, getting up at three o'clock in the morning is not much of a sacrifice. We have to be mindful that listening to other people who want to tell us what we should or should not do, can destroy our relationship and fellowship with the ones we love.

Love has even caused parents to mortgage their home for a child, even when they believed that the child had committed a crime. Whenever there is love, you will bless somebody with whatever you have, and you will lower yourself to pick someone else up. When God blesses you with someone special, you are to humble yourself to develop and strengthen loving relationships and fellowship through the Holy Spirit. Serving someone else doesn't make you less of a person; it actually makes you better.

Remember, when you humble yourself, the Lord shall raise you up. And when God raises you up, He gives you blessings so that you may have life and have it more abundantly (see John 10:10). So as Christians, we are to treat one another with the same spirit as we experience in Christ Jesus and have the same attitude as our Lord and Savior.

JESUS—IN THE FORM OF GOD

Paul takes us from having the mind of Christ to the nature and essence of Christ. Philippians 2:6 says, *"Existed in the form of God."* The words "form of God" (Gk: *morphe Theou*) refers to God's divine nature. The divine nature cannot be separated from the person of Christ because His nature and essence are Deity. What this means is that Jesus Christ possesses and expresses all of God's attributes because He is God. While Jesus was in the form of God, He was fully God, and He was fully man. E.H. Gifford concludes, "The Son of God could not possibly divest Himself of the form of God at His incarnation without thereby ceasing to be God."[1]

Paul continues in verse 8 with one of the most important passages on Christology—the kenosis, or "Christ self-emptying." Scripture shows that Christ Jesus laid aside the independent use of His divine attributes for a time. *"And being found in appearance as a man, He humbled Himself by becoming obedient to the point of death, even death on a cross"* (see Phil. 2:8). Christ Jesus divested Himself of His Deity, but withheld His pre-incarnate glory, and voluntarily restricted His use of certain attributes (e.g., omnipresence and omniscience). This is a consummate picture of Jesus Christ, as we truly understand the all sufficiency of Christ, His incarnation, and crucifixion (see Phil. 2:5-11).

It's imperative to note that when we look at the word "form," our minds immediately consider pulchritude or shape, because to us, a form is something of structure, which has definite boundaries and borders. Actually, it speaks of the shape or external appearance of a body without the essential qualities. It is the outside appearance and not what is on the inside. It may even *"holding to a form of godliness, although they have denied its power"* (2 Tim. 3:5). But God is an omnipresent Spirit, and a spirit has no shape.

So Paul is not talking about the physical shape of Christ, but of His divine essence. He is talking about a philosophical expression "form," which is an outward expression of an inward essence or character. When he said, "Jesus was in the form of God," the word "form" is an expression of "being," which carries in itself the distinctive nature and characteristic of Christ as the expression of God. Jesus is the image of the invisible God—not another god, or a part of a god. Jesus Christ is the God of the Old Testament robed in flesh. The Bible tells us, *"In the beginning was the Word, and the Word was with God, and the Word was God...and the Word became flesh and dwelt among us..."* (John 1:1,14). The Word was with God in the beginning and actually was God Himself.

It must be made crystal clear—Christ Jesus was truly one with the Father, in glory equal, majesty co-eternal. Yet He made Himself of no reputation. Jesus, in a pristine state with angels flying around Him at all levels, did something remarkable. He changed that outward expression and took on the "form of a servant" (Gk: morphe doulou). Christ Jesus with His majestic, magnanimous beauty took on the form of a servant. He gave up the manifestation of Deity, and assumed real humanity. In other words, He emptied Himself of Himself—of that divine fullness—and He willingly relinquished the glory He had with the Father before the world began. Then Jesus took out the godliness, and put on the form of a servant.

We must clearly understand that Deity was always a part of Jesus Christ, and the use of the word "form" refers to a preexisting state. It did not change when He took on the form of a man. The Matthew Henry Commentary says, "Christ not only took upon Him the likeness and fashion, or form of a man, but of one in a low state; not appearing in splendor."[2]

He became flesh and voluntarily emptied Himself and went from glory in Heaven to the profound depths of hell. It was because of love that Christ Jesus consummated His sinless obedience to the will of God by becoming obedient to the point of death, even death on a cross.

The incarnation existed in the mind of God before the world began. Scripture records, *"For He was foreknown before the foundation of the world, but has appeared in these last times for the sake of you"* (I Pet. 1:20). It is significant to note that Hegel regarded Christianity as the highest form of religion. He said, "For in Christianity, the truth that the Absolute manifests itself in the finite is symbolically reflected in the incarnation."[3]

Even though Jesus was in the form of God, expressing God, He thought it not robbery to be equal with God, because He was God. When Paul said, "thought it not robbery," there are several meanings for this word "robbery"—one is "a thing unlawfully seized"; to rob something is to take it by force. Because Jesus Christ has the form of God, He didn't walk into Heaven to take the form of God from God. We therefore conclude that He has to be God.

The second meaning is a "treasure to be clutched or retained" no matter how dangerous the circumstances are. Again, we must conclude that we can't steal the form of God from God; you can't rob God. So to be equal with God in this expression is to possess God. Jesus is the expression and nature of God.

HUMILITY AND LOVE

When you combine humility with love, you forget your ego, and do what God requires of you. You say to others, "I am here to help you develop to your fullest potential so that God can receive the glory from your life as well as from my life." So with love and humility you can say, "It is not about me." Remember, when you humble yourself, the Lord shall raise you up. And when God raises you up, He gives you blessings so you *"may have life and have it more abundantly"* (John 10:10).

Thus, being equal with God refers to the mode of Jesus Christ's existence. He willingly relinquished His glory when He came to earth, though retaining His Deity. This is now Deity having an expression, not a shape, because God is everywhere. Everywhere is formless from the point of view of shape, and everywhere is the expression of God. So far, there is no English word that can convey the word "form" any differently. It's not even possible to formulate the reality of this expression that comes from God. All we know is philosophically, God has an expression of who He is, and Jesus Christ is the expression of God.

Let's assume that all the celestial creatures, even though they don't know God's shape, understand His expression. Christ Jesus expresses God through His innate character and nature. It's the mode of the expression that is the setting of divine essence, but it is not identical with the essence itself. In other words, there is the essence, which is God (Deity), and God has an expression, which is Jesus Christ (the form of the expression). In order to have Jesus Christ (the form), you have to have the God (the Deity), but Jesus Christ (the form) is not identical with God (the Deity), even though Jesus Christ is an equal expression of God.

When we take this a little deeper, we can compare form, as if we are dealing with light from fire. The light from the fire is not the fire. As we get close to the fire, we feel the warmth, but the warmth is not the fire. The fire is giving off the expression of heat and light; but the fire is more than the expression even though the expression of heat and light are true replica of the essence of the fire. There is more to the fire than heat. There is more to the fire than light. So when talking about the form, the form and the expression are not the true essence of who Christ really is. There is more to Christ Jesus than His form and expression—Jesus Christ is Lord. Because no one can walk up to God and rob Him of His form and expression, He has to really be in the form of God to express God—*"Jesus Christ is Lord"* (Phil. 2:11).

Can you imagine God in His pristine holiness, in His celestial environment with angels, cherubim and seraphim worshiping Him? Even the spiritual creatures that don't love God have to respect Him. They have to respect Him because He is God. The following scenario may help to grasp the meaning that God is supreme and only God can be God.

In the Book of Daniel, as Daniel prayed, an angel was sent from Heaven with an answer. The Bible says, *"The prince of Persia, who is another angel, stopped the angel coming from God."* The prince of Persia stopped the angel from Heaven in his tracks for 21 days; consequently, the angel from Heaven couldn't get through to Daniel. How did he eventually get free? Michael the archangel commanded the prince of Persia to release the angel that was sent from Heaven.

When the angel with the message from God finally got through and opened his mouth, the Scripture says, "It sounded like a multitude." Can you imagine one voice sounding like a stadium of people at a football game? The Bible says that right away, Daniel's strength left him and he fell down. (See Dan. 10:8-15).

Notice that these angels can be placed on a scale by ranked order. The angel from Heaven (1st rank) had a voice like all of us together. The prince of Persia (2nd rank) stopped the angel from Heaven. Michael the archangel (3rd rank) stopped the prince of Persia. But when Michael was looking at the devil (4th rank), the Bible says, he dared not make an accusation against satan. Michael the archangel said, *"The Lord* [top rank—all power] *rebukes you"* (Jude 9).

We must realize that if Michael is this powerful, can you imagine the power of God? Jesus was in the form of God. And Jesus in the form of God was in the mode of expression that set the divine essence of who He was. Thus, the expression is not the same as the essence, because Jesus is the expression of the essential nature that shows Jesus is God.

BALANCING DEITY AND HUMANITY

Because Christ Jesus willingly laid aside His heavenly glory to come to earth and die, we should be willing to adopt Christ's attitude of love, unselfishness, servanthood, humility, and obedience, looking beyond our own interest for the sake of others.

We now know that Jesus was and is God, and that He went from the infinite heights of a pristine glory in Heaven, to the infinite profound depths of hell. He was the Word of God who became flesh and lived among men for 33 years; He was obedient to death. The Bible tells us that:

- Christ existed in the form of God.
- He was with God.
- He was equal to God.
- He became flesh.
- Even though He was Deity, He was truly man.
- As a man, He became a servant to God and man.
- He was obedient to God the Father.
- He lived a perfectly sinless life, which qualified Him to step into our place to receive the wrath of God toward sin.
- His death provided the necessary basis for redemption.

Again, we must recognize the word "form" (*morphe*). He came in the form of a servant, being made in the likeness of men. But although Jesus was in the likeness of a man, He was more than a man. His humanity was genuine, yet He was still divine. The Bible declares that the fullness of God was in Jesus from the moment of His incarnation—from the moment His human life began. Scripture clearly and unequivocally shows Jesus as God in the flesh. Prior to His incarnation, Jesus was in the form of God, and existed as essentially equal and one with God (see John 1:1-3).

As Lord and Savior, Jesus could have considered holding on to His godliness. He could have held on to the cherubim and seraphim, and all of the other things around Him. Jesus could have looked to the earth, saw mankind living in sin, and said, "I am God and I am not going to change." But when He saw us covered in sin, He refused to hold on to His godliness and let us die in our sin.

Christ shared in the glories and prerogatives of Deity, but did not regard the circumstances of His existence as something to be jealously retained. Rather, He willingly relinquished His glory when He came to earth. When Jesus took on a human form, He humbled Himself to accomplish that task for which He had come—to die for sinful humanity in order that we might have eternal life. Jesus loved us so much that He humbled and emptied Himself of His glory, and became flesh to save mankind.

ENDNOTES

1. Jeff Asher, "The Mind of Christ" Deity and Humanity of Christ, (2002), accessed 8 February 2005 available from: URL = http://www.padfield.com/2002/mind.html.

2. Matthew Henry Commentary "Philippians 2:5-11" Bible Software by Johnhurt.com.

3. "Hegel, George W. Friedrich," Microsoft (R) Encarta. Copyright (c) 1993 Microsoft Corporation. Copyright (c) 1993 Funk & Wagnall's Corporation.

CHAPTER THIRTEEN

Achieving Pristine for the Mundane

What exactly did Jesus give up when He came to earth? He gave up the expression, but He did not give up His godliness.

- He did not give up His omniscience; He is God.

- He did not give up His omnipresence; He is God.

- He did not give up His immutability; He is God.

- He did not give up His omnipotence; He is God.

Scripture says, *"He has no stately form or majesty that we should look upon Him, nor appearance that we should be attracted to Him. He was despised and forsaken of men, a man of sorrows and acquainted with grief; and like one from whom men hide their face He was despised, and we did not esteem Him"* (Isa. 53:2-3). The Son of man came not to be ministered unto, but to minister and to save (see Matt. 20:28). He renounced the glory of Heaven to suffer and die for our salvation. Indeed, what did He give up?

- He gave up the pristine—His glory, for the mundane— our sins.

- He came and subjected Himself to nine months in a woman's womb as He wrapped Himself up in panoply of flesh. He held her up while she carried Him (see Luke 1:31; Matt. 1:23; Isa. 7:14).

◆ He owned cattle on a thousand hills but was born in a manger (see Luke 2:7).

◆ He subjected Himself to hunger even while He created all the food (see Matt. 21:18; Luke 4:2).

◆ He subjected Himself to exhaustion while He was the energy of the world (see John 4:6).

◆ He subjected Himself to being questioned when He was above any question that anyone could ask (see Matt. 27:12-14; Mark 14:3-4; Luke 23:9; John 19:9).

◆ He subjected Himself to being ignored even though He had the power to cut off all oxygen.

◆ He subjected Himself to being ridiculed (see Matt. 9:24).

◆ He was spat on and cursed. They mocked Him, but He kept the servant form (see Matt. 6:67).

◆ They dragged Him through three courts and crushed a crown of thorns upon His head. They flogged Him with a flagdrum, and hung Him on a cross. Still, He was God (see Mark 15:16-20).

◆ He gave His life. He died on the Cross and was buried in a tomb.

But three days later, He rose from the grave with all power in His hands. God exalted Christ Jesus to the highest place, and He made a name for Himself.

"For this reason also, God highly exalted Him, and bestowed on Him the name which is above every name, so that at the name of Jesus EVERY KNEE WILL BOW, of those who are in heaven and on earth and under the earth, and that every tongue will confess that Jesus Christ is Lord, to the glory of God the Father"(Philippians 2:9-11).

CHAPTER FOURTEEN

Exalted to the Highest Place

After Jesus Christ was raised from the dead, God the Father restored to Him the glory that He had before His humiliation, and exalted Him to the highest place—the right hand of God the Father (see John 17:5,24; Acts 2:33; 5:31; Eph. 1:20-21). After Jesus Christ descended to the lowest depth of humiliation, God exalted Him to the highest place in eternity. God the Father also conferred on Him the name, which is supreme above every name.

The Lord Jesus Christ is the name that is above every name. The name is *Lord* [Gk: *kurios*], the Old Testament name for God. The supreme name is translated to the divine name *Yahweh*. This title of "Lord" places Him in the position of Sovereign Ruler over all things. His power and authority encompasses every age and exceeds every known power, now and in the future.

The name of Jesus Christ is far above all principality and power and might and dominion, and every name that is named, not only in this age but also in that which is to come (see Eph. 1:20-22). There are many names used in reference to Jesus Christ; common names we often use are:

- Jehovah-Rohi, my shepherd.
- Jehovah-Nissi, my banner.

- Jehovah-MKaddesh, sanctifies me.

- Jehovah-shalom, my peace.

- Jehovah-tsidkenu, my righteousness.

- Jehovah-rophe, my healer.

These are limited names in limited circumstances, but there is a name that is above every name. You know the name. It's the name of Jesus. Jesus—that's the name. That's the name we use when we ask:

- Who is this with power from on high?

- Who is this with healing in His hand?

- Who is this who can make day out of night?

- Who is this who can talk to a drug addict while he is high?

- Who is this who can take AIDS out of your blood?

- Who is this who can set you free from all kinds of sickness?

THE NAME ABOVE EVERY NAME

Because the name of Jesus is exalted over and above all creation, all things in Heaven, in earth, and under the earth will bow down and confess that Jesus is Lord. Every man, woman, and child are under the authority and rule of Jesus Christ. Even those who refuse to bend the knee to acknowledge through confession will one day acknowledge and confess that Jesus is Lord. At the name of Jesus, every knee will bow—high and low, good and bad, saved and unsaved, including satan and all his demons. *"And that every tongue will confess that Jesus Christ is Lord, to the glory of God the Father"* (Phil. 2:11).

CHAPTER FIFTEEN

Theological and Philosophical Thoughts and Concepts

THE POWER OF A HUMBLE MIND IS A MIND OF LOVE	
THEOLOGY	PHILOSOPHY
As Christ Jesus gave up His heavenly glory to come to earth in the form of a man and suffer death on the Cross, we should be willing to adopt Christ's attitude of unselfishness, servanthood, humility, and obedience; and look beyond our own interest for the sake of others. Philippians 2:3-4—*"Do nothing from selfishness or empty conceit, but with humility of mind regard one another as more important than yourselves; do not merely look out for your own personal interests, but also for the interests of others"* Philippians 2:5—*"Have this attitude in yourselves which was also in Christ Jesus"* Galatians 5:26—*"Let us not become boastful, challenging one another, envying one another"*	Philosophers have enquired whether humility is a virtue; but virtue or not, everyone must agree that nothing is more rare. The Greeks called it *tapeinosis* or *tapeineia*—"lowliness of mind." It is strongly recommended in the fourth book of the Laws of Plato: he rejects the proud and would multiply the humble.[1] John Calvin—"All the blessings we enjoy are Divine deposits, committed to our trust on this condition, that they should be dispensed for the benefit of our neighbors."[2] John Locke—"To love our neighbor as ourselves is such a truth of regulating human society, that by that alone one might determine all the cases in social morality."[3]

Romans 12:3—*"For through the grace given to me I say to everyone among you not to think more highly of himself than he ought to think; but to think so as to have sound judgment, as God has allotted to each a measure of faith"* Romans 12:10—*"Be devoted to one another in brotherly love; give preference to one another in honor"*	Saint Augustine—"What does love look like? It has the hands to help others. It has the feet to hasten to the poor and needy. It has eyes to see misery and want. It has the ears to hear the sighs and sorrows of men. That is what love looks like."[4] Aristotle—"We become just by performing just action, temperate by performing temperate things, brave by performing brave action."[5] Albert Einstein—"My religion consists of a humble admiration of the illimitable superior spirit who reveals himself in the slight details we to perceive with out frail and feeble mind."[6]

ENDNOTES

1. Plato, translator Benjamin Jowett *"Laws"* cited from Book IV, The Classis Library HTML edition, 2000, accessed 12 May 2005.

2. John Calvin, *On the Christian Life*, translated by Henry Bevridge, Institute of the Christian Religion (public domain).

3. John Locke, *An Essay Concerning the True Origin, Extent and End of Civil Government* (1690), accessed 10 March 2005; available from: http: www.cleverlely.org/areopagus/docs/locke/locke3. htm.

4. St. Augustine, *Augustine, The Confessions of Saint Augustine* (New York, NY: Bantam Doubleday Dell Publishing Group, Inc., 1960), 176.

5. Aristotle, *Lecture Notes 2* by Tom Bridges, Philosophy and Religion Department, accessed 1 May 2005; available from: www.msu.org/ethics/contentethics/lecturenotes/aristotle/Aristotlelecture.

6. Albert Einstein, *The New Quotable Einstein*, ed. Alice Calaprice, (Princeton, NJ: Princeton University Press, 2005), 195.

WORD WEALTH

Meanings and Explanations With Use and Application

EMPTIED (GK: *KENO*\KEN-O-O)
EMPTIED HIMSELF (GK: *EAUTON* KENO, SEN)

STRONG #2758: to make empty, i.e. to abase, neutralize, falsify; make (of none effect, of no reputation, void), be in vain.

VINE: "to empty," is so translated in Philippians. 2:7, "made...of no reputation." The clauses which follow the verb are exegetical of its meaning, especially the phrases "the form of a servant," and "the likeness of men." Christ did not "empty" Himself of Godhood. He did not cease to be what He essentially and eternally was.

WEBSTER: unoccupied; containing nothing; lacking reality, substance, meaning, or value; devoid of sense; marked by the absence of human life; and to remove the contents.

USE AND APPLICATION: Jesus Christ became flesh and voluntarily "emptied" (to pour out) Himself and went from glory in Heaven to the profound depths of hell.

EXISTED (GK: *HUPARCHO*\HOOP-AR-KHO)

STRONG #5225: from hupo (under) to begin under (quietly), i.e. come into existence (be present at hand); expletively to exist—after behave, live.

VINE: Primarily, "to make a beginning" (hupo, "under," arche, "a beginning"), denotes "to be, to be in existence," involving an "existence" or condition both previous to the circumstances mentioned and continuing after it. This is important in Philippians 2:6 concerning the deity of Christ.

WEBSTER: To come into being, to stand, stop; to have a real being whether material or spiritual; to have being in a specified place or with respect to understood limitations or conditions.

USE AND APPLICATION: The phrase "being (existing) in the form (morphe, the essential and specific form and character) of God," carries with it the two facts of the antecedent Godhood of Christ, previous to His incarnation, and the continuance of His Godhood at and after the event of His birth.

FELLOWSHIP (GK: *KOINONIA*\KOY-NOHN-EE'-AH)

STRONG #2842: partnership, i.e. participation, or social intercourse, or (pecuniary) benefaction: communicate, communion, distribution, fellowship.

VINE: communion, fellowship, sharing in common.

WEBSTER: to join in fellowship with a church member; to admit to fellowship (as in church).

USE AND APPLICATION: In *koionia* the individual shares in common an intimate bond of fellowship and shared in communion of Christ and the Body of Christ, as set forth by the emblems in the Lord's Supper. Fellowship (*Koinonia*) cements the believers to the Lord Jesus and to each other.

FORM(GK: *MORPHE*\MOR-FAY)
FORM OF GOD—(*EN MORPHE THEOU*)

STRONG #3444: refers to form, through the idea of adjustment of parts); shape; nature; form.

VINE: Denotes "the special characteristic form or feature" of a person or thing; it is used with particular significance in the New Testament, only of Christ in Philippians 2:6,7, in the phrase "being in the form of God," and "taking the form of a servant." An excellent definition of the word is that of Gifford: morphe is the essence form which never alters; not in the abstract, but as actually subsisting in the individual, and retained as long as the individual itself exists....Thus, morphe Theou is the Divine nature actually and inseparably subsisting in the Person of Christ....For the interpretation of "the form of God" it is sufficient to say that He partakes all the essential attributes of deity. It includes the whole nature and essence of Deity, and is inseparable from them, since they could have no actual existence without it. The true meaning of morphe in the expression "form of God" is confirmed by its recurrence in the corresponding phrase, "form of a servant." It is universally admitted that the two phrases are directly antithetical, and that "form" must therefore have the same sense in both.

WEBSTER: To give a particular shape; to shape or mold into a certain state or after a particular model.

USE AND APPLICATION: Existing as He already did in the form of God, Christ Jesus was an expression of God's divine nature and attributes because He was fully God.

GRASPED (GK: *HARPAGMOS*\HAR-PAG-MOS)
Did not regard equality with God a thing to be grasped
Gk: *Ouch harpagmon hegesato to einai isa theo*

STRONG #725: plunder—robbery, to seize, pluck, pull, take (by force).

VINE: "to seize, carry of by force," is found in Philippians 2:6, "(counted it not) a prize, "a thing to be grasped" *To be grasped*" (*harpagmos* is from a Greek word which has two meanings, "a thing unlawfully seized," and "a prize or treasure to be retained at all hazards": (1) in the active sense, the act of seizing, robbery; (2) in the passive sense, a thing held as a prize. "*Grasped*" originally meant *"a thing seized by robbery"* and eventually came to mean anything clutched, embraced, or prized, thus is sometimes translated "grasped" or "held onto." A treasure to be clutched and retained.

WEBSTER: To seize with or as if with a grapple; come to grips with; wrestle to bind closely.

USE AND APPLICATION: Christ Jesus did not regard equality with God as a *"harpagmos"*—something to be grasped "snatched" or "seized" as a robber. He did not have to retain by force His equality with God. He did not regard His being on an equality of glory and majesty with God as a prize and a treasure to be held fast, but emptied himself thereof.

HIGHLY EXALTED
(GK: *HUP.RUPS4Ç*\HOOP-ER-OOP-SAH-OH)

STRONG #5251: to elevate above others, i.e. raise to the highest position: highly exalt.

VINE: To exalt highly; is used of Christ, as in Philippians 2:9.

WEBSTER: To raise in rank, power, or character; to elevate by praise or in estimation and glorify.

USE AND APPLICATION: To raise to supreme majesty and refers to a super-eminent exaltation. Thus, the word suggests exaltation to the highest position, an elevation above all others. The context contrasts humiliation and resulting honors. Jesus' obedience to death is followed by a super-exalted position of honor and glory.

HUMBLED (GK: *TAP.IN4Ç*\TAP-I-NO-O)
He humbled himself—*heauton tapeinoo*

STRONG: #5013: To depress; to humiliate (in condition or heart; abase, bring low, humble self.

VINE: Signifies to make low; to be abased.

WEBSTER: not proud or haughty; not arrogant or assertive; reflecting, expressing, or offered in a spirit of pretense and deception.

USE AND APPLICATION: To describe a person who is devoid of all arrogance and self-exaltation—a person who is willingly submitted to God and His will.

HUMILITY (LOWLINESS OF MIND)
(GK: *TAP.IN4PHR4SUN*\TAP-I-NOF-ROS-OO-NAY)

STRONG #5012: The base of humiliation of mind, i.d. modesty; humbleness of mind, humility, lowliness of mind.

VINE: The word is a combination of tapeinos, "humble," and phren, "mind." The lowliness of mind" (tapeinos, under HUMBLE, and phren, "the mind"), is rendered "humility of mind"

WEBSTER: the quality or state of being humble.

USE AND APPLICATION: Humility is a total absence of arrogance, conceit, and haughtiness. The central thought is freedom from pride—lowliness, meekness, modesty, mildness, humble-mindedness, a sense of moral insignificance, and a humble attitude of unselfish concern for the welfare of others. Only by abstaining from self-aggrandizement can members of the Christian community maintain unity and harmony.

INCARNATION

The word "incarnation" does not appear in the Bible. It is a theological term derived from the Latin words "*in*" and "*caro*" (flesh), and it means "to be clothed in flesh." It is the act of becoming flesh. Its only use in theology is in reference to the gracious, voluntary act of the Son of God in which He assumed a human body. Christianity teaches that the Lord Jesus Christ, the eternal Son of God, became a man who had an earthly, physical, fleshly body just like yours and mine.

There is a difference between the incarnation and the virgin birth of our Lord. The incarnation speaks of the fact of God becoming man in the person of Jesus Christ. The virgin birth, on the other hand, is the method by which God the Son became man. It is the method or means by which He took on our flesh without taking on our fallen sinful nature. By means of the virgin birth He could remain sinless.

LIKENESS (GK: *HOMOIOMA*\HOM-OY-MAH)
Likeness of men—*homoioma anthropos*

STRONG #3667: A form; resemblance; made like to, likeness, shape, similitude.

VINE: Denotes "that which is made like something, a resemblance," the likeness of men." From homoioos similar (in appearance or character); denotes "that which is made like something, a resemblance," "(for) the likeness (of an image);" the AV translates it as a verb, "(into an image) made like to;" the association here of the two words homoioma and eikon "(the) likeness (of sinful flesh);" in Philippians 2:7 "the likeness of men." "The expression 'likeness of men' does not of itself imply, still less does it exclude or diminish, the reality of the nature which Christ assumed.

WEBSTER: Copy, portrait, appearance, semblance, the quality or state of being like; resemblance.

USE AND APPLICATION: Our Lord's humanity was a real likeness, not a mere phantom. But this likeness did not express the whole of Christ's nature. His mode of manifestation resembled what men are. That…is declared in the words "form of a servant." Paul justly says in the likeness of men, because, in fact, Christ, although certainly perfect Man was, by reason of the Divine nature present in Him, not simply and merely man…but the Incarnate Son of God.

NAME (GK: ONOMA\ON'-OM-AH)
The Name which is above every name—*to onoma to huper pan onoma*

STRONG #3686: A "name" authority, character, (called, surname).

VINE: is used in general of the "name" by which a person or thing is called, in Philippians 2:9, the "Name" represents "the title and dignity" of the Lord, for all that a "name" implies, of authority, character, rank, majesty, power, excellence, etc., of everything that the "name" covers.

WEBSTER: a word or symbol used in logic to designate an entity.

USE AND APPLICATION: "The Name of God" in the Old Testament, denotes the divine Presence, the divine Majesty, especially as the object of adoration and praise. The context here dwells on the honor and worship bestowed on Him upon whom this name was conferred. The conferring of this title "The Name," was upon the Lord Jesus as the Son of Man.

ROBBERY (GK: HARPAGMOS\HAR-PAG-AY)

STRONG #725: plunder, robbery.

VINE: "to seize, carry off by force," is found in Philippians 2:6, "(counted it not) a prize," "a thing to be grasped"), "(thought it not) robbery," it may have two meanings, (a) in the active sense, "the act of seizing, robbery," a meaning in accordance with a rule connected with its formation; (b) in the passive sense, "a thing held as a prize," "to set forth Christ as the supreme example of humility and self-renunciation."

WEBSTER: The act or practice of robbing; larceny from the person or presence of another by violence or threat.

USE AND APPLICATION: "Who though He was subsisting in the essential form of God, yet did not regard His being on an equality of glory and majesty with God as a prize and a treasure to be held fast, but emptied himself thereof."[1]

STRIFE AND FACTION (GK: .*ERITHEIA*/ER-ITH-I - AH)

STRONG #2052: intrigue, i.e. faction—contention, strife.

VINE: contention faction: denotes "ambition, self-seeking, rivalry," self-will being an underlying idea in the word; hence it denotes "party-making." It is derived, not from eris, "strife," but from erithos, "a hireling"; hence the meaning of "seeking to win followers," contention. It represents a motive of self-interest and is sometimes rendered selfishness.

WEBSTER: A bitter sometimes violent conflict or dissension; an act of contention; fight, struggle, exertion or contention for superiority.

USE AND APPLICATION: Faction and strife have twin meanings denoting "ambition, self-seeking, rivalry," self-will being an underlying idea in the words; hence referring to factionalism, rivalry, and partisanship and pride that prompts people to push for their own way.

VAINGLORY (GK: K.NODOXIA\KEN-OD-OX-EE-AH)

STRONG #2754: empty glorying, i.e. self-conceit: vain-glory.

VINE: "Empty conceit" (kenodoxia from kenos = empty, vain, hollow, groundless; doxa = glory, praise or opinion) is used only here in the New Testament and is translated in King James Version as "vainglory" which is defined as an excessive or ostentatious pride or "counting yourself better than others." The Revised Standard Version chose the word "conceit" to translate the Greek here. The New International Version translators rendered it "vain conceit."

WEBSTER: excessive or ostentatious pride in one's achievements; vain display or show.

USE AND APPLICATION: We speak of a vain glorious person as being conceited. "Nothing to gratify your own personal vanity" (Lightfoot); "and in search for empty glory" (Barclay). "Doing nothing impelled by empty pride" (Wuest). Note: faction and vainglory have been spoilers of the Church of God in all ages. Petty strivings for place and preferment, jockeying for advantage, pushing and shoving for prestige or attention—many congregations of believers in Christ have been blighted or destroyed by the sins Paul mentions.

ENDNOTE

I. W.E. Vine, *Vine's Complete Expository Dictionary of Old and New Testament Words* (Nashville, TN: Thomas Nelson, Inc. (1996), 251.

Practical Applications

Let this mind be in you which is also in Christ Jesus (see Philippians 2:5). Since you have been transformed by the renewing of your mind, you now have the mind of Christ. With the mind of Christ Jesus you do those things which He desires, as you think His thoughts, have His attitude, share His love, and exhibit His humility when He emptied himself. Hence, you ask yourself, "What would Jesus Do" as you ponder specific applications and reflections to apply both the theological and philosophical lessons learned in order to:

- ◆ Adopt Christ's attitude of unselfishness, servant-hood, humility, and obedience.

- ◆ Adopt attitudinal characteristics for maintaining unity and living unselfishly.

- ◆ Seek to be one in spirit with other members. The Church ought to be one in spirit because the Spirit of Christ unites the Church into one body.

- ◆ Understand the basis and importance of unity.

- ◆ Regard, consider, count, and esteem others as more important than self.

◆ Understand that giving up self for service to others is truly the power of a humble mind because humility with love brings honor and exaltation.

ACTION STEPS

A. The first step is to prayerfully read and meditate Philippians 2:1-11. As Christ Jesus willing laid aside His heavenly glory to come to Earth and die, we should be willing to adopt Christ's attitude of unselfishness, servanthood, humility, obedience and look beyond our own interest for the sake of others.

B. Think about what it means to have the mind-set of Christ. You must show evidence of selflessness and humility while considering the needs of others as your top priority.

1. Encourage and motivate others toward unity that produces joy.

2. Witness to others at home, work, while traveling, and in your daily living.

3. "Let nothing be done through selfish ambition or conceit." You are to avoid doing things with self-serving motives and discover ways to regard, consider, count, esteem, and show concern about the interests of others.

4. "In lowliness of mind you are to esteem others as being better than yourself." You are to esteem others as being more important and more worthy than you are, and be willing to accept failings in others without looking down on them.

5. "Let each of you look out not only for his own interests, but also for the interests of others." You are to avoid self-centeredness and a spirit of selfishness as you look out for the interests of others instead of being completely absorbed in your own concerns and spiritual growth.

C. Conduct your life so that others may see you as a Gospel sermon — *Let this mind be in You which was also in Christ Jesus.*

1. Be humble, and in humility think more of each other than you do of yourselves. Never act from motives of rivalry or personal vanity.

2. Cultivate a spirit of authentic Christian humility that would be evidenced by a willingness to regard others as more important than self.

3. Show and express love toward other believers and non-believers—relatives, friends, neighbors, and coworkers. You are to humble yourself, and treat them with love and dignity because it is the right thing to do.

4. Be humble, thinking of others as better than yourself. Don't be selfish; don't live to make a good impression on others.

5. Give up self for service to others—truly the power of a humble mind.

D. Read First John 3:16 and reread Philippians 2:4-8 to understand that the sacrifice of Christ is both the proof of His love and the standard of our own love for others. Then ask yourself, "Am I willing to humble myself, even sacrifice myself, in the best interest of another?"

1. Always ask yourself, "What would Jesus do?"

2. Imagine Jesus doing the things that you are doing or thinking the things that you are thinking; then reflect on how you would compare Jesus' attitude and action to your attitude and action.

E. Read John 13:3-17 to understand that Jesus' act of washing the disciples' feet demonstrated love. Jesus was their teacher and Lord, meaning He was on a higher level than the disciples, yet He assumed a position of humility and service because He loved those He served.

1. Practice being humble by serving others and committing yourself to doing things that you think are beneath you. Remember, you cannot have unity without humility, and you will not humble yourself to anybody you don't love.

2. Perform a menial task to teach a lesson in humility and selfless service because ultimately, servant-hood is a disposition of the heart and spirit, which expresses itself in concrete action.

F. Ask for wisdom to know the secret things of God. And His Spirit will reveal them to you; for you have the mind of Christ because the Spirit of Christ lives in you.

G. Read and meditate John 17:22. It is critical to understand that Christ Jesus also prayed for the future believers that they might be one.

H. Recognize that it is what you put into practice from God's Word that brings blessings to you and others.

PART FOUR

Finding Peace Through Praise

Our world is filled with anxiety, frustration, turmoil, and apprehension. There is concern for our families, finances, global terrorism, relationships, and a multitude of other matters, for which all seek peace. Yet peace often remains an elusive stranger that we long to befriend.

Contrary to what many people think, peace is not a mind over matter. You cannot talk your way into peace. Rather, it is when you take your eyes off yourself, your circumstances, and your world, and focus them on God that you will discover peace. In this section, you will discover that you can praise your way into peace.

When you begin to see yourself and your world through the eyes of God, you will tap into tranquility and true happiness. Once your thoughts have been transformed so you focus vertically rather than horizontally, then peace like a river will flood your soul.

CHAPTER SIXTEEN

Rejoice Always

Think praise. In Philippians, God has commanded that we are to "rejoice always" and to think on things that give us peace, consolation and victory, in spite of the circumstances we face in our lives. Accordingly, we find that the apostle Paul, though a prisoner, was exultantly happy, and calls us to be full of joy and to rejoice always.

As we carefully read and review Philippians, we find that there is a connection between rejoicing and the power of the mind. In chapter 2 of Philippians Paul tells us to *"have the mind of Christ"*; and as he is about to close, he says in chapter 4, *"Finally brethren, think on these things."* It appears that the power to think is the antibody, the antidote to anything that can happen in one's life.

There is no question that when Paul says, *"Rejoice in the Lord always. Again I will say, rejoice!"* he is not asking us to rejoice at certain times or in certain circumstances, he is commanding us to rejoice at *all* times. He detaches rejoicing from our circumstances as he sends out a carte blanche statement, an imperative command, "Rejoice and again I will say rejoice." Without knowing what situations we will face and without conducting a survey, Paul sees us (with his spiritual eyes) hesitating and contemplating how to rejoice in negative situations. It is clear that he feels the need to repeat himself because of our hesitation. Essentially, he is saying, "Just in case you didn't hear me the first time, I will say it again—I want you to always give God an expression of jubilee. Rejoice and again I will say rejoice."

Paul says it again and again because we need to hear it again and again. We need to know that the joy of the Lord is so powerful; it can abound even in the worst situations. It is imperative for you to understand that it does not matter what you have, or what is happening in your life, you must know within your heart that you are special and that God indwells your mind through His Spirit.

Since you are connected to God through His Spirit you can rejoice as you look through the eyes of faith to see that God has planned for you to praise, to worship, and to thank Him for His faithfulness, no matter how devastating the circumstances, because *"the joy of the Lord is your strength"* (Neh. 8:10). The joy that comes from the Lord is what gives you ability and strength to overcome trials and to realize victories, and to refuse to yield to what the flesh wants to do even when we're faced with discouraging circumstances. The Holy Spirit tells us that our circumstances are not to dictate our attitudes; rather, our praise claims that God is above the situation, and rejoicing becomes a lifelong occupation.

What does it mean to "rejoice always"? The word *rejoice* is an imperative, a command that comes from the word *joy*, a fruit of the Spirit. To rejoice is the central core of why we were created. God created us to give Him glory, and we are expected to always have joy as we give Him praise. Richard Baxter said, "May the Living God make these, our carnal minds so spiritual, and our earthly hearts so heavenly, that loving Him, and delighting in Him, may be the work of our lives."[1]

Yes, Christians are commanded to rejoice under all circumstances, and obedience is possible because true joy is in the Lord. As believers, we can be inwardly joyful when everything around us is dreary. This means that you are to rejoice even when the doctor tells you that the diagnostic report reveals cancer in your body. Why? You rejoice and praise God for the healing process that is taking place in your body.

You rejoice and praise God for overcoming the chemotherapy and radiation. You rejoice and praise God for the surgeon, anesthesiologist, nurse, orderly, medication, and everything that will be used for your treatment and complete healing. You rejoice and praise God because you have been transformed by the renewing of your mind, and you now have the mind of Christ. You look past the suffering to victory in healing, and you boldly declare, *"I know how to get along with humble means, and I also know how to live in prosperity; in any and every circumstance I have learned the secret of being filled and going hungry, both of having abundance and suffering need. I can do all things through Him who strengthens me"* (Phil. 4:12-13).

Paul's attitude teaches us an important lesson. Our inner attitudes do not have to reflect our outward circumstances. Paul was full of joy because he knew that no matter what happened to him, Jesus Christ was with him. So when we encounter situations in which there seems to be no reason for happiness, we can always rejoice and delight in the Lord.

Similarly, in Second Corinthians 6:10, Paul encouraged us to be joyful: *"As sorrowful, yet always rejoicing; as poor, yet making many rich; as having nothing, and yet possessing all things."* Rejoicing is to be a constant discipline for those who are in Christ because we are aware that Jesus gives peace to those who trust Him and ask for His help. Moreover, true faith never says, "I cannot." We have the freedom to rejoice always. More importantly, we rejoice always because God has delivered us from the corruption and death in sin, and we have the promise that the Lord Jesus is coming soon.

Habakkuk also reminds us that when the circumstances of life present a negative picture of failure and loss, or when the natural reaction is grief or complaint, this is the time to put faith in God and in His Word.

> *"Though the fig tree should not blossom and there be no fruit on the vines, though the yield of the olive should fail and the fields produce no food, though the flock should be cut off from the fold and there be no cattle in the stalls, yet I will exult in the LORD, I will rejoice in the God of my salvation"* (Habakkuk 3:17-18).

Thus when you ask, "How can I rejoice when life seems to be crushed by persecution, failures, negative experiences, or horrific circumstances?" You can rejoice and praise God at the same time you are fighting the sinful nature of the flesh with the will of the spirit because the Spirit of Christ, the Living Water, is constantly flowing through your transformed and renewed mind. You can praise God that you have the victory over the devil because you have been released and you now have the mind of Christ.

ENDNOTE

1. Cited in *Inspirational Christian Quotes by the Puritans and Other Great Reformed Theologians*, accessed 18 September 2005; available from: http://www.eternallifeministries.org/quotes.htm# Promises%20of%20God.

Chapter Seventeen

You Are What You Think

Who are you? It is what you think about yourself that gives significance to who you are. What you think about yourself can elevate or decline your position. When you understand the equation of the thinking process, you will know that you are your thoughts, and your thoughts are somewhere within you. Thus, self-knowledge becomes significant to overall knowledge; and it is in the mind where you store what you think about yourself.

The question then is: Can someone be thinking of praising God, while at the same time, not thinking of joy and rejoicing? It does not seem possible, because when you deal with the concept of the mind, you cannot be separated from what you think, and you cannot think separately from yourself. Moreover, it is significant to understand that the mind is attached to the source, which is the power of God; while at the same time, the mind is also connected to the flesh—the body, and the body is connected to your environment, issues, and circumstances.

What Is the *Mind*?

Remember that in the Old Testament, the word *mind* was translated from the Hebrew word *nephesh*, which means the total person—soul, spirit, and mind. Moreover, the words *mind* and *spirit* were often interchanged because the mind serves almost the same function as the spirit. In the New Testament, the Greek word used in this text for "mind" is *nous*, which is defined by *Strong* as "the intellect, the mind in thought, feeling or will; the understanding." *Nous* is further defined as the total conceptual process of thinking. In essence, your mind is more than your brain, your thought, your intellect, or your reason; it is the whole conceptual process that begins with the spirit that resides at the core of your being, and ends with the life actions that are produced in the soul. In other words, your mind not only includes the conception or the creation of an idea, your mind causes you to act according to what is being produced in your spirit—your soul.

According to Descartes, dualism began as an awareness of listening to the soul, the still center and spiritual experience when he captured this profound self-awareness in the famous words, *Cogito, ergo sum*: "I think, therefore I am." Descartes then proceeded to develop his epiphany into a formal philosophy, which we now call Cartesian dualism. Modern philosophical theories of the mind are based on scientific understanding of the brain; and the *mind* is seen as a phenomenon of psychology. The term is often used more or less synonymously with consciousness.

More importantly, using your mind is rooted in biblical precept; in the New Testament the believers are encouraged to:

- ◆ Love your God with all your heart and with all your soul and with all your mind in each of the synoptic Gospels (see Matt. 22:37, Mark 12:30; Luke 10:27).

- ◆ Be of one mind (see Acts 4:32, I Cor. 1:10; 2 Cor. 13:11).

- ◆ Be transformed by the renewing of your minds, which is a process. In First Corinthians 14:15, Paul says that he will pray with his spirit and also with his mind; he will sing with his spirit and also with his mind.

- ◆ Come now, let us reason together, says the Lord.

Likewise, the Old Testament tells us *"For as he thinks within himself, so he is"* (Prov. 23:7). The heart is symbolic of the mind, and your mind is who you are; your mind is the real you. It is therefore unrealistic to think that you are to rejoice only during pleasant circumstances, and to worry or be anxious regarding issues and situations that are unpleasant or painful. It is also unrealistic to determine, "I am not suppose to think about a bad situation or an impending crisis"; for when danger presents itself, the mind must recognize it, whether it's spiritual or sensual (sinful in nature), and evaluate what must take place.

YOUR MIND EVALUATES YOU

The mind is a place of evaluation; and in order to evaluate, you must be objective about subjective things. Your mind should rise above your thoughts as your spirit tells you what to do in all circumstances. Your mind must stay free in order to make judgments about who you are, what to do, where to go, and what to wear. Aristotle said, "In the soul which is called mind, that whereby the soul thinks and judges."[1] Your mind should be free from the contamination that makes it turn against you, because your mind is the only thing you have to protect you from your environment. You need to keep your mind free so that you are constantly aware of dangerous issues and circumstances that may come close to your body, mind, and spirit.

You should always reject negative thoughts from your mind because these thoughts will destroy you. When you think seriously about this, it is even better to allow poverty, sickness, or other uncontrollable circumstance to create problems in your life than for you to allow your mind to turn against you and eventually destroy you.

Good thoughts will ultimately lead to good thoughts about yourself, and bad thoughts will ultimately lead to bad thoughts about yourself. So when you are having problems with your circumstances, sooner or later it comes around to you. The more negative you think, the more negative you become. And when you become negative, you reduce yourself rather than flourish; and ultimately, your thoughts become your greatest enemy. You cannot remain a positive person while thinking negatively.

It is therefore imperative that you understand that your mind is too powerful for you to allow it to turn against yourself. You can't afford to let your mind turn and work against you. You need your mind to fight the environmental battles, to stave off the evil spirits, to be a conduit for the power of God, to bring out your creativity and to offset the negativity of your environment. You can't afford to think negativity in a negative situation. You are not to think yourself into sickness, poverty, non-productivity, and non-creativity. You have to think your way out of it.

The command is that we are to worship and rejoice in the Lord always. Notice Paul uses the perfect tense when he says, *"Be anxious* [careful] *for nothing."* (See Phil. 4:6.) He is actually saying, "Don't continue to be anxious [careful] for anything." He is telling us to thank and praise God in the middle of our trials, because when we praise, we release our trials and tribulations to God.

PRAISE RELEASES

Praise releases us; but negative condemnation, including negative thought and criticism, restricts and controls us. You must, therefore, be very careful to allow the spiritual mind to maintain control over negative thoughts that are being fed from the carnal mind or mind of the flesh, which is connected to the world through your senses.

It is also good to know that as you are rejoicing and praising God, He is washing your minds of your trials and tribulations as He gives you the peace of God. When you release the negative thoughts, the Spirit of Christ guards you with His peace.

ENDNOTE

1. Aristotle, *On The Soul,* by Chase B. Wrenn, cited from *Internet Encyclopedia of Philosophy,* accessed 18 June 2005; available from http://www.iep.utm.edu/.

CHAPTER EIGHTEEN

Don't Worry, Be Happy

We have often heard the question, "Why worry when you can pray?" You may also remember the song, "Don't worry, be happy." We are not to worry because worrying is a device of the devil. When we worry, we are saying that we don't trust that God will provide our needs. Most of us worry about things that will never happen or things that are of very little significance. We worry that we don't have the right kind of clothing. We worry about being with the right person; then we worry that we do not have a new car or enough money in the bank. Some of us even worry because we can't control other people.

Paul uses the perfect tense to tell us not to worry, but to worship instead. He says, *"Be anxious for nothing, but in everything by prayer and supplication, with thanksgiving, let your requests be made known to God."* The word "but" suggests a bold and strong contrast from *"Be anxious for nothing* [don't worry]*"* to the command to *pray*. The little word "but" cancels the first part of the statement—"Be anxious for nothing" or don't worry about anything.

Clearly, there is a definite connection between Philippians 4:6 and 4:8. Verse 6 says, *"Be anxious for nothing, but in everything by prayer and supplication, with thanksgiving, let your requests be made known to God."* And verse 8 says, *"Finally, brethren, whatever is true... if there is any excellence and if anything worthy of praise, dwell on these things"* Verse 6 is a positive instruction against negativity, and verse 8 tells us that we are to fix our thoughts—think on things that are true, honorable, right, pure, lovely, admirable excellent, and worthy of praise.

Prayer now replaces worry for the Christian believers; prayer is an antidote to worry. In essence, prayer combats worry by allowing us catharsis—spiritual renewal by purging our emotions, eliminating stress, releasing tension, and bringing us into expressions of praise, thanksgiving, and joy.

FAITH AND PRAISE

Because worry and prayer cannot coexist, we must choose to be contented in all circumstances, pray in faith about what we need, and praise God for all He has done. There is clearly a relationship and spiritual connection between faith and praise—we are dealing with the substratum issues of the child of God, who is connected to God by faith; it is a spiritual connection. Two key points for us to remember are that faith is based on knowledge of God's Word and His character; and the spirit of the world is in opposition to God. Thus, when we stand in faith, the world loses its controlling influence over our minds.

The Hebrew word for "faith" (*emeth*) connotes faithfulness, which equals "trusted," "trustworthy," or "confidence and trust in God and in God's Word." It does not mean belief in a dogmatic sense. In the Greek, however, the word for "faith" is *pistis*, and primarily conveys firm persuasion, confidence, assurance, trustworthiness, or a conviction based upon hearing. Faith is, in general, the persuasion of the mind—that a statement or idea is true and worthy of trust. To understand this concept more clearly we refer to the Bible passage, *"Now faith is the assurance of things hoped for, the conviction of things not seen"* (Heb. 11:1).

The writer of Hebrews provides a description of how faith works, instead of a definition of faith. The author stresses that faith is established conviction concerning things unseen and settled expectation of future reward. Faith is the title deed of things hoped for; and throughout

Hebrews chapter II the author emphasizes that assurance rests on God's promises. For example, *"that Christ may dwell in your hearts through faith. . .to know the love of Christ which surpasses knowledge"* (Eph. 3:17-19). The love of Christ in its fullness is beyond all human comprehension, and not even the greatest minds of theology and philosophy can explain an understanding of God through reason and experimentation. It is only by faith that we come to know the love of Christ Jesus. Also, Romans 10:17 states, *"So then faith comes by hearing and hearing by the word of Christ."* Yet faith is not something that we produce; it is what God's Word produces in us.

The Bible is clear, Christ Jesus is our spiritual leader, and it is by faith that we follow Him. He tells us, *"If anyone wishes to come after me, he must deny himself, and take up his cross, and follow Me"* (Mark 8:34). We are the sheep of His pasture, and we hear and know His voice as He speaks to us. We also know that Christ is the perfecter of our faith; and while on the cross, He said, *"It is finished!"* (John 19:30).

PRAYER RELEASES WORRY

As Paul reminds us that we should not be anxious about anything, we can shout these words of victory. The Greek word for "anxious"— *merimnate*—refers to concern that may become fretful and inappropriate if taken too far. Paul tells us that instead of being anxious and becoming distraught over a particular situation, we should take it to the Lord in prayer. Matthew 6:25-34 illustrates the worthlessness of worry by showing that it is unnecessary, unfruitful, and unbecoming to a Christian:

> *"For this reason I say to you, do not be worried about your life, as to what you will eat or what you will drink; nor for your body, as to what you will put on. . . . Look at the birds of the air, that they do not sow, nor reap nor gather into barns, and yet your heavenly Father feeds them. Are you not worth much more than they? And who of you by being worried can add a single hour to his life? . . . So do not worry about tomorrow; for tomorrow will care for itself. Each day has enough trouble of its own"* (Matthew 6:25-34 NKJV).

You can thank and praise God because you are connected to the Spirit of Christ, whom you can pray to, instead of worry. Prayer now replaces worry.

Paul used several different Greek words for prayer in this verse. "Prayer" (*proseuche*) is the most general term for our communications to God. "Supplication" or "petition" (*deesis*) refers to requests for particular benefits. "Thanksgiving" (*eucharistias*) is grateful acknowledgment of past mercies. "Requests" (*aitemata*) looks at individual requests of God that form part of the whole prayer.

Supplication is more than petitioning; it also suggests an intensity of earnestness in extended prayer—not to gain merit by many words, but to fully transfer the burden of one's soul into God's hands. Prayer and peace are closely connected. One who entrusts cares to Christ instead of fretting over them will experience the peace of God to guard him from nagging anxiety.

Don't worry; pray. The word for "prayer" here is *procekee*, and it means prayer as worship. Part of the antibody for worry is worship. With faith and prayer, we place our problems and worry into God's hands. Once your mind evaluates and determines a problem, you are to put the problem into God's hands. When you raise our hands in worship, you are to release anything that causes you to worry. Paul says, prayer is stressing a sense of need; prayer with a supplication request stresses thanksgiving for the object asked for. So when you worship and make your requests, we should immediately praise Him for the object of request. When you praise and worship Him, you release the cares of your mind to the One who is all-powerful. When you come to God, you free your mind from the negative. You ask Him for what you need, and praise Him for giving it to you as you allow your minds to dwell on those things that will give you the victory.

CHAPTER NINETEEN

Praise Brings Peace That Transcends Understanding

Prayer and peace are closely connected. When you pray, you can push back the attack of your circumstances and your situation, defeat the tormenting thoughts in your mind, and claim the victory in order to experience peace of mind. If you pray rather than worry, God will give you peace, which transcends all powers of thought.

As for letting your requests be known to God, C.H. Spurgeon said:

> Cast your trouble where you have cast your sins; you have cast your sins into the depth of the sea, there cast your trouble also. Never keep a trouble half an hour on your own mind before you tell it to God. As soon as the trouble comes, quick, the first thing, tell it to your Father. Remember, that the longer you take telling your trouble to God. The more your peace will be impaired.[1]

In order to keep your mind focused on God, trusting in Him, you need to spend time in daily fellowship with Him. Isaiah declared unto God, *"The steadfast of mind You will keep in perfect peace, because he trusts in You"* (Isa. 26:3).

THE PEACE OF GOD

The phrase "the peace *of* God" is peace that comes from God rather than peace *with* God. It is important to note that one may have peace with God without having the peace of God. Peace *with* God is dependent upon faith, whereas peace *of* God is a promise, which is the result of a thankful prayer to God. It is peace that comes to us—the tranquility of God's own presence—when we pray.

The peace of God actually describes your relationship with God. This peace is different from the world's peace. It is the peace that Jesus promised His disciples and all those who follow Him: *"Peace I leave with you; My peace I give to you. not as the world gives do I give to you. Let not your heart be troubled, nor let it be fearful"* (John 14:27). In Romans 5:1 Paul writes, *"Having been justified by faith, we have peace with God through our Lord Jesus Christ."* It is essential you understand that true peace comes from knowing that God is in control and not just from positive thinking. As believers, we have *"the peace of God, which surpasses all comprehension will guard* [keep] *your hearts and minds through your Christ Jesus"* (Phil. 4:7).

The Greek word for "guard," *phroureo*, is a military term that means to surround, protect and keep a garrison or city. It is similar to soldiers standing guard, patrolling or protecting a sentry or sanctuary against the enemy. You are in spiritual combat, guarded and protected by God's power and peace as your sentinels or patrols, surrounding the perimeter of your mind. Whenever or wherever there is a weak spot or area in your mind, God's peace is the soldier that guards that part of your mind so you can think positively in all circumstances. Thus, when the enemy attacks with a negative thought, the sentry guard moves to that position in your mind and begins to shut out every destructive thought from the devil. The peace of God counterattacks so we begin to think positively.

Remember, *"who are protected by the power of God through faith for a salvation ready to be revealed in the last time"* (1 Pet. 1:5). You should always be aware that God's peace completely surrounds your heart, mind, emotion, appetite, soul, and spirit in order to secure you against satan's attacks and other harmful outside forces. And when you are thinking of the good things He has done, you will want to give Him thanks and praise.

GIVING THANKS AND PRAISE

Even though you may think you have no reason to thank Him, the Bible says to do so. *"always giving thanks for all things in the name of our Lord Jesus Christ to God, even the Father"* (Eph. 5:20). We give thanks because He is working everything together for our good (see Rom. 8:28).

It is His will that we give thanks: *"In everything give thanks: for this is God's will for you in Christ Jesus"* (I Thess. 5:18). You are to begin with thanksgiving. *"Be anxious for nothing; but in everything by prayer and supplication with thanksgiving let your requests be made known unto God. And the peace of God, which surpasses all comprehension, will guard your hearts and your minds through Christ Jesus"* (Phil. 4:6-7).

Philippians 4:7 (AMP) states, *"And God's peace [shall be yours, that tranquil state of a soul assured of its salvation through Christ, and so fearing nothing from God, and being content with its earthly lot of whatever sort that is, that peace] which transcends all understanding shall garrison and mount guard over your hearts and minds in Christ Jesus."*

You can praise and thank God in all things and in all circumstances because *"God's peace shall be yours."* When you think of pure things, just things, lovely things, righteous things, honest things, and things of good report, you move to praise and thanksgiving.

As Christian believers, we are connected to the Spirit of Christ, possessing the peace of God which guards us from worries and anxieties. And with the peace of God, our minds are free to think praise. When we think praise, God keeps us in perfect peace because our mind is stayed on Him and because we trust in Him. Consequently, your future will be better than your past because peace in the heart will follow praying about your concerns.

Most of us have experienced lack of peace from time to time when we pray. Paul was not saying that you will feel absolutely at ease and relieved after you pray. Still, a measure of peace will be yours. You will have the confidence that you have laid the matter before the Lord and you trust Him. Note that he does not promise peace as the indicator of God's will when you are praying about what you should do. Paul did not say that if you need to make a decision God will make His will known by giving you peace about the right choice.

Once the joy arises, and joy is what we feel toward God, it brings us to place of praise, and when we praise and rejoice in the midst of trials, we then release those trials and tribulations to God. As we do so, we release the negative thoughts and begin to think positively. When we rejoice and praise God, He guards our mind with His peace. So when we thank and praise God, our minds are washed and renewed in order for the peace of God to mount against our sinful desires.

Because God has connected our mind to His creative power, we must recognize from a personal point of view that every child of God has to become more spiritual in his or her thinking. It is significant then to understand that becoming spiritual in your thinking does not make you a religious fanatic; rather, it brings you into a closer relationship with the Spirit of God. Thus, you ought to keep your mind on the One who can do more for you than you can do for yourself. That's spiritual thinking.

It is critical to remember that because you have been transformed by the renewing of the mind, your thoughts are now connected to praise and glory. Praise is not dependent upon your feelings or emotions, it is: *"I will give thanks to the Lord, with all my heart"* (Ps. 9:1). *"I will bless the Lord at all times; His praise shall continually be in my mouth."* (Ps. 34:1). We are to always rejoice and think praise.

Paul reminds us that through praising and rejoicing we have been transformed by the renewing of the mind; and with our renewed minds we are identifying God as being above our situations as we worship God in Spirit and truth. It is through our worship that we are able to identify God for who He is and what He does. You are transformed by the renewing of your mind.

REASONS TO REJOICE

You are now "out of the box," and you can boldly proclaim, "I am now liberated and free; no longer trapped in the box of negative and destructive thinking." We give God praise because He has loved us so much that He gave His only begotten Son, and because of His blood, we have been washed into righteousness.

When you are connected to the Spirit of Christ, you can personally say:

- I have the desire and the will to be creative, victorious, and the best I can be.

- I must not allow my thoughts to overpower my will.

- I will not allow others to control my will by controlling my mind or my thoughts.

- I can do all things because the Spirit of Christ has renewed my mind.

- I can now change my circumstances.

- I am a child of God. The Lord Jesus is my Savior, and I belong to Him.

- I am in Christ and not under condemnation.

- I am healed, delivered, and set free.

- I am transformed, and I have a renewed mind.

You *rejoice* because you have the mind of Christ, and with the mind of Christ, you can say, *"The Spirit of the Lord GOD is upon me, because the LORD has anointed me to bring good news to the afflicted; He has sent me to bind up the brokenhearted, to proclaim liberty to captives and freedom to prisoners; to proclaim the favorable year of the LORD"* (Isa. 61:1-2).

Giving up self for service to others is truly the power of a humble mind because humility with love brings honor and exaltation. The humiliation and exaltation of Christ are lessons for all believers: "As Christ ceased not to be a King because He was a servant, nor to be a lion because he was like a lamb, nor to be God because He was made a man, nor to be a judge because He was judged; so a man does not lose his honor by humility, but he shall be honored for his humility."[2] Does your life demonstrate a Christ-like humility that God will delight to honor by exaltation? If so, then you can boldly proclaim:

- I am beautiful, extraordinary, magnanimous, and very special to God.

- I am blessed and anointed.

- I am rejoicing and praising God at all times.

- I have the mind of Christ, and the Spirit of Christ dwells in me.

- I think like Christ; I am a winner.

- I can win all mind games through Christ who strengthens me.

- Rejoice and again I say rejoice.

We are to:

- *Rejoice* because Christ Jesus loved us and he laid down His life for us.

- *Rejoice* because we are redeemed from sin with the precious blood and sacrificial death of Christ.

- *Rejoice* because God gives us His love that surpasses all understanding.

- *Rejoice* because Jesus said, *"If you loved Me, you would rejoice because I said, I am going to the Father, for My Father is greater than I."*

- *Rejoice* and be exceedingly glad, for great is our reward in Heaven.

- *Rejoice in the Lord!*

ENDNOTES

1. C.H. Spurgeon, *Prayer Perfumed with Praise*, The Spurgeon Archive, April 1879, accessed 9 April 2005; available from http://spurgeon.org/sermons/1469.htm.

2. John MacArthur, *Christ Humbled/Christ Exalted*, *The Exaltation of Christ – Part 1*; (Tony Capoccia Bible Bulletin Board, Columbus, NJ, 1986), accessed 18 June 2005; available from http://www.biblebb.com/files/MAC/sg50-17.htm.

CHAPTER TWENTY

Theological and Philosophical Thoughts and Concepts

REJOICE AND BE CONTENTED IN ALL CIRCUMSTANCES.
Never lose the power to think on things that give you peace, consolation, and victory in spite of the circumstances you face in your life.

THEOLOGY	PHILOSOPHY
Be full of joy…rejoice! It seems strange that a man in prison would be telling a church, people who are free, to keep on rejoicing. He stresses to them the joy that they ought to have because of their relationship with God. Paul was full of joy because he knew that no matter what was happening in his life, he would be free if he kept his mind on Christ Jesus. Scripture is clear—we are to never lose the power to think on things that give us peace, consolation, and victory in spite of the circumstances we face in life. Philippians 4:4—*"Rejoice in the Lord always. Again I will say rejoice!"*	Saint Aquinas—"Man cannot live without joy; therefore when he is derived of true spiritual joys it is necessary that he become addicted to carnal pleasures."[1] Aristotle—"Suffering becomes beautiful when anyone bears calamities with cheerfulness, not through insensibility but…." "The ideal man bears the accidents of life with dignity and grace, making the best of circumstances."[2] Kant—"It is not God's will merely that we should be happy, but that we should make ourselves happy."[3]

Luke 10:20—*"but rejoice that your names are recorded in heaven."*

Romans 12:12—*"Rejoicing in hope, persevering in tribulation, devoted to prayer."*

Romans 15:13—*"Now may the God of hope fill you with all joy and peace in believing so that you may abound in hope by the power of the Holy Spirit."*

Galatians 5:22—*"But the fruit of the Spirit is love, joy, peace."*

Philippians 2:17-18—*"But even if I am being poured out as a drink offering upon the sacrifice and service of your faith, I rejoice and share my joy with you all. You too, I urge you, rejoice in the same way and share your joy with me"*

Colossians 1:11-12—*"strengthened with all power, according to His glorious might, for the attaining of all steadfastness and patience; joyously giving thanks to the Father"*

Colossians 1:24—*"Now I rejoice in my sufferings for your sake."*

Spurgeon: "Trials teach us what we are; they dig up the soil, and let us see what we are made of."[4]

"Thee Lord gets his best soldiers out of the highlands of affliction."[5]

Calvin—"There is not one blade of grass, there is no color in this world that is not intended to make us rejoice."[6]

Marcus Aurelius: "When you arise in the morning, think of what a precious privilege it is to be alive—to breathe, think, to enjoy, to love."[7]

Pascal—"The strength of a man's virtue should not be measured by his special exertions, but by his habitual acts."[8]

Calvin—"You must submit to supreme suffering in order to discover the completion of joy.[9]

Martin Luther—"No man ought to lay a cross upon himself, or to adopt tribulation…but if a cross or tribulation come upon him, then let him suffer it patiently, and know that it is good and profitable for him."[10]

C.S. Lewis—"Some people feel guilty about their anxieties and regard them as a defect of faith but they are afflictions, not sins. Like all afflictions, they are, if we can so take them, our share in the passion of Christ."[11]

ENDNOTES

1. St. Thomas Aquinas, *The Summa Theologica: Treatise On Grace*, (Benziger Bros., 1947), accessed 20 March 2005; available from www.ccel.org/a/aquinas/summa/FS/FS109html.

2. Aristotle, "Aristotle on Friendship," *Nicomachean Ethics Book 8*, Chaper 1.

3. Immanuel Kant, *The Critique of Practical Reason – The Philosophy Page*, accessed 1 February 2005; available from: http//www.philosophypages.com/ph/kant.htm.

4. Charles Spurgeon *"Sermon Notes 242,"* accessed 22 February 2005; available from: http://www.sovereign-grace.com /spurgeon-sn/chsn024.htm.

5. Ibid.

6. John Calvin, *On the Christian Life*, translated by Henry Bevridge, *Institute of the Christian Religion* (public domain).

7. *Quotes from Brainy Quotes*, accessed 1 March 2005; available from: www.brainyquotes.com.

8. Blaise Pascal, *Pensees* (London, England: Penguin Group), 224.

9. John Calvin, *BrainyMedia*, 2006; available from: http://www.brainyquote.com/quotes/quotes/j/john-calvin182893.html.

10. Martin Luther, *The Freedom of a Christian World Civilizations, An Internet Classroom and and Anthology* (Washington State University, 1996), accessed 1 February 2005; available from: http://www.wsu.edu:8080/~dee/REFORM/FREE-DOM.HTM>.

11. C.S. *Lewis Quotations* by C.S. Lewis, Famous Quotes–Word Power, accessed December 2005; available from: http://wordpower.ws/quotations/c-s-lewis.html.

Word Wealth

Meanings and Explanations With Use and Application

NXIOUS = CARE (GK: *M.RIMNA*\MER-IM-NSH)

STRONG #3308: to divide, "the mind." The word denotes distractions, anxieties, burdens, and worries.

VINE: Signifies to be anxious about, to have a distracting care.

WEBSTER: characterized by extreme uneasiness of mind or brooding fear about some contingency: Worried resulting from, or causing anxiety.

USE AND APPLICATION: means to be anxious beforehand about daily life. Such worry is unnecessary because the Father's love provides for both our daily needs and our special needs.

PRAISE (GK: *EPAINOS*\EP-AHEE-NOS)

STRONG #1868: superimposition, as a relation of distribution. Laudation, a commendable thing: praise.

VINE: Denotes "approbation, commendation, praise" it is used of those on account of, and by reason of, whom as God's heritage, "praise" is to ascribed to God, in respect of His glory (the exhibition of His character and operations), of whatever is praiseworthy.

WEBSTER: An expression of approval; commendation; worship; to glorify (a god or saint) by the attribution of perfections.

USE AND APPLICATION: Epainos expresses not only praise for what God does for us, but also for who He is, recognizing His glory.

PRAYER (GK: *PROSECHUE*\PROS-YOO-KHAY)

STRONG #4335: prayer (worship); by implication, an oratory prayer.

VINE: Denotes prayer to God, "to ask" should make a request. Also, (Gk. "deesis") primarily "a wanting, a need, "an asking, entreaty, supplication."

WEBSTER: An address (as petition) to God or a god in word or thought.

USE AND APPLICATION: It is important to note that the word prayer has several meanings and uses. Starting with noun, (Gk. *"euche," "proseuche," "deesis," "eneuxis"*) which are prayers to God that also includes making a vow, the word expands to the verb (Gk. *euchomal*), a special term describing an invocation, request, or entreaty. Adding pros, "in the direction of God, (Gk: *proseuchomal*) becomes the most frequent word for prayer.

REJOICE (GK: *CHAIRO*\KHAK´-EE-RO)

STRONG #5463: To be cheerful, i.e. calmly happy or well-off; salutation (on meeting or parting), be well; farewell, be glad, God speed, greeting, hail joy, rejoice.

VINE: "To rejoice; rejoicing in the Lord and in His presence; the rejoicing of others.

WEBSTER: To give joy; to gladden; to feel joy or great delight.

USE AND APPLICATION: *Chairo* describes a joy is rejoicing and to rejoice is to be glad or be gratefully happy.

Practical Applications

"REJOICE IN THE LORD ALWAYS"

We are commanded to rejoice under all circumstances, and obedience is possible because true joy is in the Lord; and we must refuse to worry about things because Christ Jesus gives peace to those who trust Him and ask for His help.

We are to put into practice lessons learned from theology and philosophy in order to:

- Rejoice and be contented in all circumstances. This joy is to be experienced *always*.

- Understand that rejoicing is a constant discipline.

- Understand that we rejoice because true joy is in the Lord.

ACTION STEPS

A. Prayerfully and carefully read the Book of Philippians (only four short chapters). This book is truly a masterpiece full of tenderness, warmth, affection, joy, and rejoicing.

B. Memorize Philippians 4:4-7 and allow the truth of the text to order your thinking and your life. The ultimate purpose is for you to love God with your mind, and to trust Him at all times.

Rejoice in spite of trials.

1. Pray and thank the Lord for taking you through this situation.

2. Praise God for who He is and what He has already done for you.

3. *"**Praise** the Lord for the Lord is good; sing praises to His name, for it is lovely"* (Ps. 135:3).

4. *"**Sing** for joy to God our strength; shout joyfully to the God of Jacob."* (Ps. 81:1).

If you have done something you should not have done, or not done what you should have done, then you are to:

♦ Confess your sin because, "If we confess our sins, He is faithful and just to forgive us our sins and to cleanse us from all unrighteousness."

♦ Pray as though everything depends on God; at the same time, you are to do all that you can to change the situation.

Rejoice in the joy of others. Rejoice when others are blessed and honored.

1. Let your gentleness be known to all men. The Lord is at hand. Everyone who comes into contact with you should experience gentleness, moderation, and patience.

2. Show respect for family members and close friends, not just the people you're trying to impress spiritually.

3. Be gentle and kind to everyone and practice saying nice things to friends, family, and strangers.

4. Give a word of encouragement and show appreciation for the little things.

5. Be responsible and let other people know that they can depend upon you.

Reasons to rejoice and offer praise.

1. *Rejoice* because God commands that you are to rejoice always.

2. *Rejoice* because Christ Jesus loves you and He died for your salvation.

3. *Praise* God verbally for who He is and what He has done.

4. Remember, God's written Word is always relevant, powerful, and alive. The Word says, *"**Rejoice** in the Lord always. Again I will say **rejoice**."* Don't forget the word *"always."*

5. Believe that God loves you and He will never leave you. Knowing that God loves you and that He wants to communicate with your spirit gives you the strength to carry on—no matter what difficulties you are facing. Just knowing that *"the joy of the Lord is your strength"* will bring peace and comfort at all times and in all circumstances.

6. When you encounter a situation that is stressful or difficult and you don't feel happy, you can still be joyful on the inside as you rejoice and delight in the Lord.

Additional copies of this book and other
book titles from DESTINY IMAGE are
available at your local bookstore.

Call toll-free: 1-800-722-6774.

Send a request for a catalog to:

Destiny Image® Publishers, Inc.

P.O. Box 310
Shippensburg, PA 17257-0310

*"Speaking to the Purposes of God for this
Generation and for the Generations to Come."*

For a complete list of our titles,
visit us at www.destinyimage.com